Aeneas MacDonell Dawson

The Catholics of Scotland from 1593 and the Extinction of the Hierarchy in

1603

Vol. 4

Aeneas MacDonell Dawson

The Catholics of Scotland from 1593 and the Extinction of the Hierarchy in 1603
Vol. 4

ISBN/EAN: 9783743349162

Printed in Europe, USA, Canada, Australia, Japan.

Cover: Foto ©Lupo / pixelio.de

Manufactured and distributed by brebook publishing software (www.brebook.com)

Aeneas MacDonell Dawson

The Catholics of Scotland from 1593 and the Extinction of the Hierarchy in 1603

CAP. LIV.

PRINTING THE NEW TESTAMENT—NO CHANGE OF MEANING—3000 COPIES OF THE OLD TESTAMENT—BISHOP DOUGLAS AND OTHER ENGLISH CATHOLICS SUBSCRIBE—THE COUNT D'ARTOIS AT EDINBURGH—MISSION FUNDS HELD IN TRUST BY BISHOP CHISHOLM, SOME PRIESTS AND TWO LAYMEN—BONAPARTE AT THE GATES OF ROME—AN ARMISTICE—PEACE ON HARD CONDITIONS—PRINCE AUGUSTUS—HIS LOVE FOR THE SCOTCH MISSION—PROVIDING FOR THE SAFETY OF THE POPE DURING THE PANIC—IN 1797, BISHOP GEDDES WORSE—BISHOP HAY'S CONCERN—AQUORTIES LEASED FOR A COLLEGE—A HOUSE FOR 30 STUDENTS BUILT—SUPERSEDED BY BLAIRS—ITS CONDITION IN 1835—NOW ALMOST A SOLITUDE—ABERDEEN-SHIRE FRIENDLY—IN 1797, THE FRENCH ONCE MORE APPROACHING ROME—FLIGHT THE ONLY HOPE—THE POPE'S HORSES IN HIS COACH WHEN A BRITISH OFFICER CAME TO ANNOUNCE THAT THERE WAS NO IMMEDIATE DANGER—IMPORTANT ANNUAL MEETING AT GIBSTON—BISHOP HAY VINDICATED—STATE OF THE MISSION FUNDS—THE CONGREGATIONS URGED TO ASSIST THEIR PASTORS—COADJUTOR APPLIED FOR—SEMINARY FOR THE HIGHLANDS—PAINFUL CONDITION OF BISHOP GEDDES—SECOND SIGHT.

By October, 1790, Bishop Geddes and Mr. Robertson had fairly begun to print the New Testament. The Greek and Vulgate versions, three English Catholic translations, King James' and the Italian version of Martini, which had been commended by the Pope, were all before them. They were so sparing in making alterations, that in the whole Gospel of St. Matthew, which they had gone through, they had not changed the meaning of one word. Some expressions, indeed, they had changed. Bishop Challoner had done the same in every one of his three editions. It does not appear that the work of reprinting was continued; nor are we informed as to the amount of work that was done. Nothing practical was accomplished, apparently, till the year 1796, when Bishop Hay, in concurrence with others, bargained with John Moir, a printer at Edinburgh, for an edition of 3,000 copies of the Old Testament, in four volumes. The total expense, including paper and binding, was £740. Bishop Gibson subscribed for upwards of 1,000 copies in sheets, Bishop Douglas for 600, Mr. Thomas Eyre at Crookhall, for 100, and Coghlan, the bookseller, for 100. Moir printed a like edition of the New Testament at £197. The two English Bishops took 1,350 copies, Mr. Eyre, 100, and Coghlan, 100. The selling price of the Old Testament bound, was 12s.; that of the New, to nonsubscribers, three shillings. The work was undertaken and paid for by subscription. Half of the price was to be paid on delivery of the second volume. By this means alone money was obtained for printing the remaining volumes. Payments to workmen and for paper required to be made regularly. Neither the Bishop nor Mr. Moir had capital to advance for that purpose. The former, nevertheless, was under the necessity of advancing upwards of £80 in order to complete the work. The Bishop remained in Edinburgh the greater part of the summer, superintending the press.

Early this year, the exiled Count D'Artois came to Edinburgh. He was most hospitably received; and apartments were fitted up for him in the Palace of Holyrood. It was his intention to remain there, until it should be possible for him to return to France, as heir to the Crown. Bishop Hay was introduced to him by his chaplain and was graciously received.

The Bank of Scotland making a call on its shareholders, at this time it became necessary that Bishop Hay should pay to the bank as much as £1800. This would oblige him, he said, to live, at least six years, with the greatest economy. Bishop Geddes had great doubts as to the expediency of lodging so much money in the bank in one name. It was a subject he thought, for deliberation and advice, on account of the umbrage it might give to some ill-inclined persons, that Bishop Hay should have so large a sum of money in the bank, both on account of the inconvenience of transferring so much property in case of the Bishop's death, and of the temptation it presented to his relations in the event of any informality or error in his possession. Inquiry, even, in such a matter would be disagreeable.

As soon, accordingly, as Bishop Hay could proceed to the North after attending to the printing of the Scriptures, the two Bishops executed a trust deed of all their properties in favour of Bishop Chisholm, of some of the clergy and two lay gentlemen whom they enpowered in the event of their decease without successors to hold in trust all the monies standing in their names, for the interests of the mission.

At this time, Rome was panic-struck by the approach of a French army under Bonaparte. It had taken Bologna, and was marching in three columns by different routes, against the City of the Popes. The Roman army was quite unable to make head against this formidable force, being only 3,000 in number, and consisting chiefly of the most undisciplined soldiers that could be imagined. Two-thirds of them were French emigrants, Italian deserters and the refuse of other nations. Diplomacy was at work; but, meanwhile, the fear of the French soldiery prevailed. The Scotch agent, writing to the Bishop, says: "Such noise and confusion there was in town, such dejection and despair surpasses all conception; not a house but resounded with the cries of women and children; not a countenance but expressed terror and dismay, many entirely lost their judgments, and parents attempted to make away with their daughters by a violent death to preserve them from insult. If the courier who came to announce an armistice had delayed for twenty-four hours more, scenes would have happened here that would have equalled anything that is barbarous in history, and it is too probable that this day Rome would be a mass of ruins. Glory to God the danger is over, and I trust there is no fear it will recur. We have made an armistice; and a plenipotentiary is despatched to Paris in order to conclude a peace. The conditions are dreadful and humiliating to the last degree. We have ourselves to blame for them."

Before the courier arrived the more religious people betook themselves to prayer. Their miserable army gave them no hope; and the terror inspired by the enemy that was so near their gates, was greater than would be caused by a horde of the worst barbarians. Every street was crowded with penitential processions at all hours of the day, and even the night. Prince Augustus had not left Italy.

During the panic he advised the Scotch agent to fly with his young charge. As for himself he declared that as long as there was any chance of his being of service to the Scotch mission, in Rome, he neither could nor would fly. Mr. McPherson, the Scotch agent, has made arrangements for sending his students to Naples or Tuscany. The Irish agent had disappeared. Mr. Smelt, the English agent, was resolved to seek safety in Naples. The Cardinals also determined on taking refuge in the kingdom of Naples, carrying the Holy Father along with them; for they were convinced that if he fell into the hands of the French they would certainly convey him to Paris, where every bad consequence, both as regarded his safety and the welfare of religion, was to be dreaded.

In January, 1797, Bishop Geddes became suddenly worse. Bishop Hay set out, at once, to close, as he believed, the eyes of his friend, and coadjutor. The invalid, however, rallied, once more; and the Bishop continued his journey to Fetternear in order to confer with Mr. Leslie, the proprietor, on the lease of a farm for the seminary. An amicable arrangement was speedily made. The Bishop obtained a lease of the farm of Aquorties on the banks of the River Don, two miles from the House of Fetternear and three from the town of Inverurie, for 107 years.

The farm consisted of 200 acres of arable land and 400 of hill and moor. The rent was £120, or £90 yearly, £500 being paid on taking possession. It was resolved to commence immediately the building of a house for the seminary, and at the same time the requisite farm offices. It was an arduous and costly enterprise. Hence it was necessary to solicit subscriptions. The congregation of Propaganda was first applied to; but, owing to the distracted state of Italy, could give no assistance. The Government was appealed to in favour of the work through Sir John Hippisley. The Catholics of the Lowlands subscribed more largely than could have been expected. Mr. Bagnal, the young priest of Kirkconnell, obtained from his congregation alone more than £80. Edinburgh subscribed £120. Aberdeen and the neighbouring country the same amount. Other missions contributed in proportion. The house, not including out buildings, cost £1,000; not a large sum, considering that it was calculated to accommodate thirty students, together with the requisite number of masters and servants.

It was still occupied by the mission when the writer visited the place, the year of his ordination, 1835. The late Rev. James Sharp was at that time in charge of both the farm and the congregation. A later visitor found it, when in the hands of a stranger, quite undivested of its college-like appearance. The building is of solid granite, three stories high, with an attic, eighty feet in length by twenty-two in width. It faces the South, and the River Don in all its beauty is seen from the front windows. Its pleasure garden, although not large, is finely ornamented with shrubberies and a small pond. It is surrounded by a formal belt of trees and presents a fair specimen of the landscape gardening of the period. At the western end of the building is the chapel, about twenty feet by fourteen, and rising to the height of the second story. An outside door admitted the congregation. There are galleries at the sides and each end of the chapel. In that which faces the altar there were seats for the Fetternear family and a few people besides. In another gallery on the epistle side of the altar, communicating with the school-room, the students had their seats. The altar and altar rails were still preserved as they had been originally, the worthy tenant, acting on the impression that a place once dedicated to divine worship should not be subjected to meaner uses. The Corinthian pillars above the altar still supported a canopy. The space on the floor of the chapel had been for the service of the congregation. At the back of the house there is a large and fruitful kitchen-garden. It was first set apart by the Bishop and cultivated according to his directions. It is still kept in the highest order. The Bishop had a room in the house to which he resorted in his declining years; and in this room he departed to the better world. The place, hallowed by so many interesting associations, is now comparatively a solitude; and in thinking of what it was and what it is, one is reminded of the lines of Rogers:

> "Mute is the bell that rung at peep of dawn,
> Quickening my truant feet across the lawn;
> Unheard the shout that rent the noontide air,
> When the slow dial gave a pause to care.
> Up springs at every step to claim a tear,
> Some little friendship formed and cherished here;
> And not the lightest leaf but trembling teems
> With golden visions and romantic dreams."

Sir John Hippisley, who was now residing at Warfield Grove, Berks, took a warm interest in the new seminary. As much aid was required in establishing it, and the Bishops contemplated applying to the Government, Sir John advised that they should address Mr. Dundas and, through him, the Duke of Portland. The worthy Baronet himself also undertook to recommend the matter to Government, and for this purpose desired to have a statement of the least possible expense that would be required to commence the seminary. The assistance of the English Catholics might also be requested.

It was now admitted that a long lease, such as the Bishop had obtained, was preferable to a purchase of property, so little could the Catholics, as yet, rely on the better feeling towards them that had come to prevail in the country. It was, indeed, a disadvantage that there were but few Catholics in the neighbourhood of Aquorties. But such disadvantage was counterbalanced by the fortunate circumstance that the Protestant population of Aberdeenshire were more friendly to Catholics than that of any other part of the country. The agent at Rome did all in his power to interest in the cause of the new seminary the Cardinals Gerdil, Albani and Antonelli. They favoured it with their approbation; but, in the uncertain state of affairs in Italy, they did nothing more.

In February, 1797, the French were once more at the gates of Rome. There was the greatest consternation in the city. It behoved the Scotch agent to provide for the safety of the students. Acting under the directions of the Cardinal Protector, he secured the ready money and church plate of the college and made arrangements for the departure of the few students there and of fifteen English students whom their agent had left to do as they best could. He was much assisted by Mr. Graves, an English merchant at Rome. Passports and everything else that was required, being procured, the party left Rome for Civita Vecchia on 12th February. Mr.

Sloane, a Scotch merchant there, was all attention to them. The day before their departure eleven Cardinals fled from Rome. The Pope's horses were in his coach, and he was himself dressed for flight, when a British officer, Colonel Duncan, arrived at the Vatican from Florence, and gave information to the effect that the danger was not so imminent. The Holy Father shed tears when he found that it was not necessary to leave his capital so suddenly. In the course of a fortnight the British students came back to their colleges. The agent was not, as yet, however, without apprehension; but he gave way to importunity.

The annual meeting was held this year at Gibston, near Huntly. Bishops Hay and Chisholm met there in the month of August, the administrators of the mission funds. It was an important meeting. Bishop Hay thereat adopted measures that effectually put a stop to the reports injurious to his character as an honest manager of the mission affairs, which were afloat ever since the last meeting of administrators which was held three years previously. Regarding the partial appropriation of a legacy to a special purpose, his opponents had accused him of acting without the advice or concurrence of the administrators, and of endeavouring to force them, in an overbearing manner, to do as seemed to him fit in the matter.

The second question concerned an extraordinary supply voted for division among the clergy. The Bishop had been accused of arbitrarily excluding some of them from the benefit of this supply, contrary to the known intentions of the administrators. In order to meet these accusations, the Bishop laid before the meeting a detailed statement of all that occurred at the former meeting and extracted therefrom a number of queries to which he requested categorical replies. This request was complied with ; and the replies, completely clearing the Bishop of all that had been alleged against him, were written down by Mr. John Reid, clerk to the meeting, and signed by all the administrators present. Thus were the ill-judged and unfounded misrepresentations of Mr. Farquarson and a few others who thought themselves aggrieved by the Bishop, completely, publicly, and finally refuted. At the same meeting Bishop Hay resigned the office of procurator, Mr. Charles Maxwell succeeding. Mr. Maxwell, in consequence, removed from his mission at Huntly to Edinburgh. The income of the mission was much reduced by the complete failure of its funds in France and a great falling off in the remittances that usually came from Rome. Four hundred and nineteen pounds yearly, was all that could be relied on while the expenditure for *quotas*, that is the allowances to the priests alone, amounted to more than £550. The guardians of the fund, therefore, were under the painful necessity of issuing a circular letter informing their brethren why they were compelled to reduce the quotas to £15 for the large towns and £10 for country missions.

Hitherto the Catholic laity had not considered it a duty to contribute towards the support of their pastors. They were now addressed on the subject in a document signed by the Bishops and appended to the letter which conveyed to the clergy the unwelcome tidings that their miserable salaries must be reduced. The people were shown that there is high authority for requiring that they should contribute towards the maintenance of their clergy. They were told, moreover, that unless they made an effort in this direction, all pastoral ministrations must necessarily cease.

The usual letters to Rome were signed later by Bishop Geddes at Aberdeen. In these letters the Bishops renewed their request for a coadjutor in the Lowland District (a request which, as has already been shown, was complied with), and informed the Cardinals that it was the intention of the Bishop of the Highland District to establish ere long, at home, a seminary, similar to that which had been already so auspiciously begun by his brother Bishop of the Lowlands. It was also intimated that Bishop

Geddes had nearly lost his speech, that his appetite was gone, and that, from time to time, he was attacked with such violent internal pain as to make it difficult to believe that he could live an hour. His patience, meanwhile, was most exemplary.

The meeting once over, a new matter, on which the reader will be glad to have the opinion of the Bishops, came up for consideration. It was quite natural that Bishop Chisholm should be applied to for information on the subject of second sight, which was more prevalent in the Highlands than in any other part of Scotland. The agent at Rome, Mr. McPherson, requested of him answers to certain queries, and with such answers the Bishop readily supplied him. In a letter of 19th August, 1797 Bishop Chisholm wrote:

"1st. It is my own private opinion that such a thing has existed and does now exist, though less frequently than in former times. Many are fully convinced of the real existence of the 'second sight;' but, many likewise, look upon it as a chimera. But you will observe that many are incredulous in matters of greater consequence, and many know nothing about the matter, and many are ashamed to acknowledge their belief on this head, as the belief of the second sight is not fashionable.

"2nd. There are treatises written on the second sight.

"3. Some families are more famous for the second sight than others; such is the family of McDonald of Morar, though it cannot be said to be confined to any particular family exclusively.

"4th. The nature of it is generally a short and sometimes imperfect representation of what is to happen, does happen, or has happened at a distance beyond the reach of natural knowledge.

"5th. Such as are affected with the second sight, see indiscriminately, happy and unhappy events, but more frequently, events of black and melancholy complexion. They see them before the event takes place, while it takes place, and after it has happened, but at such a distance that it would be impossible to know it so soon in a natural way.

Forbes of Culloden, President of the Court of Session, while employed in checking some of the Highland Chiefs from joining the Prince, was cast by contrary winds into one of the small western isles. He went, as he landed, to a gentleman's house, who had a snug elegant dinner prepared for him and his company on their arrival. "Sir," said the President, astonished at the sight of the entertainment, and understanding the gentleman,s fortune could not be great, "May I beg leave to ask if you always live in this style." "No, my Lord," says the landlord, "that I cannot afford." "And how," replies the President, "did you happen to have such a dinner to-day?" "I knew," said the Islander, that your Lordship was to be here to-day," "Impossible," answers the President, "we only landed just now, and, a little before, we knew nothing about it ourselves." "Why, my Lord, a man who lives by me announced your arrival by describing your Lordship's person, your company, dress, figure, etc., and informing me of the time you would be here to-day, which made me prepare the dinner you see."

A connection of mine, Major Chisholm, son to Chisholm of Chisholm, was one day, as he told me, walking with his father before the door of the latter's castle, when from the castle, a woman, famous for the second sight, rushed out and cried aloud: "God preserve your son, Laird, God preserve your son Roderick, I see him all covered over with blood." In a short time who appeared on an eminence coming home but Roderick supported by two men, and all covered with blood, after a dangerous fall which was only a prelude to the blood he spilt soon after, under the Prince, while he commanded his father's men at Culloden. After receiving a mortal wound, my uncle who was next in command to him, wanted to remove him from the field, and made a motion to follow him. "No," said he, "command the men lest any of them should leave the ranks."

Bishop Hugh McDonald's servant fainted, one day, at table. When he recovered he was asked the cause: "Why," said he," I saw a dead child on the table before me." Within a little space the dead body of the child was stretched on that very table. The Bishop told the story.

Bishop John McDonald's nephew, who was bred in England, came to see his friends in the Highlands. While in Morar, among some of his relations, he was, all at once, struck. When asked about it, " I see," answered he, " a person drowned, taken out of the water ;" and he described his appearance. In a short time after, the accounts of such a man as he described being drowned and taken out of the water, were received. I knew the man.

A short time before you (Mr. Paul McPherson) went to Rome, (1793), in my vicinity while in Strathglass, a child saw his father, Bailie Hector McKenzie, steward to McKenzie of Seaforth, in the winding sheets. His father called him his little prophet, and soon after, died.

You have now the second sight brought down to your time from Culloden. I could, for the information of their Lordships, give you my opinion relative to the cause of it; I do not mean a natural cause ;

but, as this has not been asked, I refer it to another time. Some, in very pompous expressions, have attempted to explain the second sight in a natural way; but their accounts appeared to me most unsatisfactory and absurd. I ever am, my dear sir, unalterably yours,

JOHN CHISHOLM."

CAP. LV.

SECOND SIGHT CONTINUED—ALEX. CAMERON, BISHOP—REGARDING A BRITISH RESIDENT AT ROME—MISSION OF BALLOCH—THE BISHOP REJECTS UNNECESSARY CHANGES — WOULD HAVE CHURCH MUSIC BUT FOR THE TEMPER OF THE TIMES—THE MUNSHES PRIEST'S DOCTORS OF DIVINITY—BRIGANDAGE OF FRENCH SOLDIERS—PIUS VI. HURRIED AWAY FROM ROME—CONVEYED TO VALENCE—DIED THERE 29TH AUGUST, 1799, AGED 81—SCOTCH COLLEGE SEIZED BY FRENCH REPUBLIC—REV. P. MACPHERSON BRINGS STUDENTS SAFELY HOME—MR. MACPHERSON HIGHLY HONOURED IN LONDON—ASTONISHMENT IN POLITICAL CIRCLES—BISHOP HAY JUBILANT.

The question of second sight appears to have been a good deal studied at Rome. One of the Cardinals wrote a treatise on it; and while engaged in collecting facts and materials for this work, Bishop Hay took great pains in supplying him with cases that had occurred, chiefly in the Highlands; and such only as were well authenticated. The Cardinal's object was to show that the *faculty of second sight* originated with the evil spirit. The Bishop held the same opinion as the Cardinal as to the origin of the *faculty*. Regarding the fact of its existence, there could be no question. There were two instances, particularly, which he was wont to relate, giving the proofs, the names of the parties, places, witnesses, etc. The first of these was that of a man, possessing the *faculty of second sight*, who declared that he saw a child, at the time in apparent health, running about the house, dressed in its grave clothes. In the other case was described circumstantially, the accidental death of a man, at the time of the vision in perfect health.

The Rev. Donald Carmichael combated the Bishop's opinion which ascribed the faculty to the agency of the evil one. How could the devil know such and such future contingencies? The Bishop's reply was that although the devil has no absolute knowledge of the future, he might have seen in the case of the child some indications of internal and mortal disease, not yet apparent to human perception. In the case of the man, the devil might have prepared the accident and made a pretty sure guess as to the event, even though it was no more than a guess or a conjecture. It would be interesting to know what the Bishop thought of the Lord President's case, related above in Bishop Chisholm's letter. Nothing short of *absolute knowledge* of the future which he denies, and which we must all deny to the evil one, could have enabled him through a seer, to give notice of the President's arrival at the house of the gentleman where he dined so well. If the arrival was brought about by the power of the devil, he must, once at least, have mistaken his vocation when he refrained from wrecking the boat and drowning the learned judge and excellent man, together with his whole company. This would have been more in keeping with the character which Scripture gives to the fiend, who "goes about like a raging lion seeking whom he may devour." (*Sicut leo rugiens, quærens quem devoret.*)

It was arranged that the newly appointed coadjutor should be consecrated in Spain. The first news which he had of his appointment was in a letter from Mr. McPherson that reached him at the same time as an official intimation from Bishop Hay, written at Huntly. The Bishop was kind and complimentary. The agent's letter was also very gratifying, and the more so as Mr. Cameron cherished a warm friendship for the Scotch agent at Rome and all his former associates. Mr. Cameron's promotion caused a vacancy in the Rectorship of the College of Valladolid. The Scotch Bishops, desiring to avail themselves of the privileges granted by a former King of Spain, Charles III., prayed that his successor, Charles IV., continuing the same privileges, would name to the office one of three whom they proposed. They, at the same time, commended the College to His Majesty's favour.

About this time Sir John Hippisley informed Bishop Hay, that but for the irruption of the French into the Papal States, a British resident at Rome would have been appointed by the British Government. In the actual circumstances, however, there was to be only a Resident on the part of the British Merchants, in the person of Mr. Graves. No assistance had, as yet, been obtained from Government for the Scotch Mission. The worthy Baronet was still watching for an opportunity to forward the matter.

There was some rather warm discussion between Bishops Hay and Chisholm in regard to the Balloch or Drummond Mission, where Mr. Andrew Carruthers was placed. It does not appear to have led to any important result; and hence no details need be given.

Mr. Robertson, the Benedictine friar from Ratisbon, desired the sanction of the Bishop to some unnecessary and inappropriate changes which he had introduced into the services for his small congregation at Munshes. He wished that English prayers, and long ones too, should be enjoined on all congregations before Mass; that the sermon should be delivered in the middle of Mass instead of being always preached before Mass began, as had been the custom in the Scotch mission from time immemorial, and that there should be music in his chapel. The Bishop patiently reasoned with him on all these points; and firmly refused to sanction such unnecessary changes. It would be appropriate and edifying to have suitable church music, the Bishop always thought, but the temper of the times must be considered. Mr. Robertson's way of managing his congregation was very peculiar. A set of people called *Elders* formed his council, respecting the poor; there were lecturers and Psalm readers in the chapel on Sundays, and the council met at the village of Dalbeattie once a week, to discuss points of faith and controversy. At these councils he sometimes presided himself; if not perhaps Thomas Copeland, John Rigg, (two tenants,) or some such Doctor of Divinity took the chair. Such like practices led to the opinion which came to prevail in the country, that Mr. Robertson's prayers were not like those at Terreagles and Kirkconnell. Mr. John Pepper, the Chaplain at Terreagles, who first gave this information in a letter to Mr. C. Maxwell, expressed the opinion that a hard task was in preparation for Mr. Robertson's successor.

As the occupation of Rome by the French affected the interests of the Scotch Mission, allusion to it here is not out of place. What the Romans dreaded for some time, fell upon the city with all its terrors. A French General, Duphot, happening to be killed in a riot which he himself excited, no better pretext was required by the Revolutionary Army. It was commanded by General Berthier, and unceremoniously entered and took possession of the city. It acted, however, with what, for such an army may be called moderation. There was neither pillage nor massacre; and, as long as Berthier commanded, discipline was tolerably well maintained. The mean and cruel Massena soon succeeded, when there occurred serious disorders. The houses of noblemen and other wealthy citizens were entered and objects of value carried off. Such brigandage touched the honour of the army; and the indignant officers presented to the General a strong and determined remonstrance, to which were affixed several pages of signatures. Massena, in order to counteract this formidable opposition to thievishness, ordered a considerable portion of the army to quarters at some distance from Rome. The officers refused to obey; on which, Massena resigned the command and left the city. A greater robbery, meanwhile was remorselessly committed. The Holy Father was deprived of his temporal sovereignty, and deported, successively, to Sienna, the Chartreuse (Carthusian Convent) of Florence, Parma, Turin, Besancon in France, Grenoble, and, finally, Valence, where Pius

VI., exhausted by fatigue and anxiety, ended his days on the 29th of August, 1799, aged 81. The people, wherever he passed, were loud in their demonstrations of affection and veneration.

Three days after the removal of the Pope, the Scotch College was taken possession of in the name of the French Republic; but not without much show of civility. Mr. McPherson, the agent, remained a month longer, hoping to do something still for the service of the mission. His chief care, however, was the safety of the students. It is very noticeable that the French authorities gave him money for his and their journey, together with a passport through France and a letter to the Minister of the Interior, in case they should get into trouble. Mr. McPherson's charge was a heavy one; but he acquitted himself of it with complete success. By 7th April, he had reached Genoa; and there, as well as at Civita Vecchia, he met with the greatest civility on the part of the French authorities. A few weeks later, he completed, without accident, the journey which he had so courageously undertaken, travelling from Marseilles through the heart of France, with his youthful charge to London.

In London Mr. McPherson was much honoured. He was an object of interest to His Majesty's Ministers, to all of whom he was introduced by Sir John

Hippisley. He had interviews with the Speaker of the House of Commons, and presentations to the Prince of Wales and the Duke of York. The whole political world was stirred by the presence of a man who had so fearlessly undertaken and successfully performed a journey which to all appeared exceedingly dangerous. Men's admiration was all the greater as they still retained but too lively a recollection of the worst atrocities of the French Revolution. Mr. McPherson, himself, was very cool over the matter, and only hoped that the acquaintance of so many great people would prove useful to him on some future occasion. Bishop Hay's anxiety was relieved, it was "a cordial to his heart," he said, to receive the agent's first letter from London, intimating his safe arrival. He immediately communicated the good news to Aberdeen and other places.

CAP. LVI.

VALUABLE MANUSCRIPTS—MR. MACPHERSON'S RETURN TO SCOTLAND—KIND LETTER OF CARDINAL GERDIL—PASTORAL LETTER ON LOYALTY---BISHOP GEDDES' LAST LETTER—REVOLUTIONARY PRINCIPLES SECRETLY SPREADING IN SCOTLAND—PROPERTY OF THE SCOTCH COLLEGE, ROME—ST. PETER'S AND THE JEWS—SIR JOHN HIPPISLEY IN BEHALF OF MISSION FUNDS—PUBLIC MEN FAVOURABLE—GOVERNMENT GRANT—LETTER OF MR. DUNDAS—THE FRENCH TEMPORARILY DRIVEN OUT OF ROME, BUT TOO SOON AS YET TO RESTORE ANYTHING—HOME SEMINARIES—LAST ILLNESS AND DEATH OF BISHOP GEDDES—HIS WRITINGS—PROPAGANDA ROBBED—AIDED BY A LIBERAL SPANIARD—AUSTRIANS AND RUSSIANS BEAT THE FRENCH—SAWARROW UNDERSTOOD TO HAVE COMMISSION TO DELIVER THE POPE—PIUS VI. CONVEYED TO VALENCE—DIES THERE.

Mr. McPherson brought from Paris, four valuable manuscripts, the property of the Scotch College there. He lent them to Mr. George Chalmers, the eminent antiquary, who, in return, gave the agent a carefully written receipt. It contains the titles of the manuscripts which had belonged to the Archbishop of Glasgow. They are also enumerated as follows: 1st, Of the Chartulary of that See (Glasgow) marked A; 2nd, The Chartulary of the same, marked B; 3rd, An Original Register in paper of the Lands and other Temporal Rights of that See; 4th, Another Register in paper, marked on the outside, 1499, 1510, also concerning the Temporal Rights of the same See. Then follows a promise to return the manuscripts on demand, and a most polite acknowledgment of Mr. McPherson's kindness. It happened unfortunately when Mr. Chalmers died, that the Chartulary marked A, and the Register of the Lands of the See of Glasgow, notwithstanding the receipt, were considered as his private property. The other two manuscripts are now at Preshome together with other historical treasures.

Mr. McPherson now returned to Scotland, where, as may be well conceived, he met with a cordial welcome. Bishop Hay had need of this consolation, for he was overwhelmed with grief when he heard that Rome was in the hands of the French Revolutionists and the Holy Father their prisoner.

The agent was the bearer of a most kind and consoling letter from Cardinal Gerdil to the Scotch Bishops.

Bishop Hay, after visiting the building operations in progress at Aquorties, set about preparing a pastoral letter on the Duty of Loyalty to the Government. As usual, he took counsel on the subject with his invalid coadjutor, requesting him to give a sketch of the general plan of the letter. Bishop Geddes replied by an amanuensis, at great length, notwithstanding the severity of his ailments. It was the last letter that he ever composed. From this date, the afflicted Bishop no longer took any part in public affairs, but, turning his face away from the world, thought only of preparing for the final change, which, he believed, was near at hand.

The pastoral letter on Loyalty was speedily issued from the Edinburgh Press; and was well calculated to meet a want of the time; for there is no denying that the dangerous principles of the French Revolution were secretly spreading even among the cool and wary population of Scotland.

All the moveable property of the Scotch College at Rome was sold, and the College itself, together with the Church was let. Mr. Sloane bought from the Jews the pictures that were in the Church and the *pietra sacra* (altar stone) of the high altar. These objects it was his intention to restore in more happy days. Meanwhile he was proud to have them, as he stated in a letter to Mr. McPherson, particularly his "friend St. Andrew," which art judges pronounced a good picture, and also "St. Margaret." a work which he intended to have repaired. It was not to be supposed that at such a time even the great Church of Rome and the Catholic world should escape being desecrated. St. Peter's was to be closed and delivered during four months to the Jews to be ungilded; and then it was to be given to the Capuchins. The Church, however, was partially saved by the parsimony of the Jews. They would not pay the price demanded for the gilding, and so the vandalic operation of removing it was not performed.

The robberies in Italy and France had so much reduced the funds of the Scotch mission that there was only a very inadequate allowance to the priests for maintenance. This was a great hardship, especially in the poorer missions. The very friendly and indefatigable Sir John Hippisley was much moved by the statements made to him by the Bishops, and resolved to use his great influence with His Majesty's Ministers in order to obtain a grant from the Government in aid of the clergy. All his diplomacy was put in requisition, and it needed it all. The Ministers were friendly and inclined to bestow the desired grant; but they dreaded lest by so doing they should raise a storm of fanatical intolerance, for they well knew that this kind of demon was not dead, but only slept. Mr. Dundas, indeed, distinctly expressed his fear in a conversation with Sir J. Hippisley ; whilst, at the same time, he admitted that a good case had been made out for relieving the Scotch clergy. Sir John was not to be defeated. He drew up an amended statement, in which it was suggested that some private persons in Scotland might be named to whom Government might hand over a sum of money for the relief of the Catholic clergy ; and that the persons so entrusted should pay this money to the Bishops for the benefit of their clergy. The proposal was pleasing to Mr. Dundas ; and the papers relating to it were left with him. There was still much negotiation. The Lord Advocate wrote to Bishop Hay, in his own hand, although it was his custom to dictate to a clerk, stating that he was directed to ask the Bishop's opinion of the following scheme of relief, and to invite any amendments, or alterations that might occur to him. Government proposed to give each of the two Bishops £100 a year ; each of the two coadjutors £60 ; and to each of the fifty clergy £20 a year. Bishop Hay was asked whether he would wish a distinction to be made between the Bishops and their coadjutors, whether the Bishop first in rank should have more than his colleague, say £120, and the second £90 or £100 ; and the coadjutors in a similar proportion; and whether the £1000 which the Government designed for the clergy of the second order should be divided equally among them all. As to the "schools" the Bishop's letter of February 26th, on which this scheme was based, did not state, explicity, what amount of aid was necessary to preserve them in the same state, as before their continual losses. Their funds were stated to be thirty shares of bank stock and £800 capital, equally divided between the two "schools." The Bishop was now asked to say whether more than this was required for their efficiency, and how much more. As to the two Colleges which were then in progress of erection, the same inquiry applied. "Your own good sense and discretion," the Lord Advocate concluded, "will, I am sure, dictate to you the delicacy of this last topic and the unavoidable necessity of these two establishments being kept on as private and limited a footing as is consistent with the object of the undertaking." When the Bishop's answer should arrive, the Advocate trusted to be able, ere long, to inform him "that a class of persons whose virtue and loyalty I so much respect, as I do that of the Catholic clergy and laity of Scotland, are relieved by the liberality of the British Government from the distresses under which they have been so unfortunately subjected." The business was finally settled at an interview held by both the Scotch Bishops with the Lord Advocate at Edinburgh (June 17). Each of the Bishops was to receive £100 a year, and his coadjutor £50. It was also settled that the Government allowance to the clergy should be at such a rate, as, when combined with the income of their common fund, should give each priest £20 a year. The new Colleges were to receive, each of them £50 a year, and each of them also, a grant of £600 towards their erection.

The Bishops could not but be grateful to the Ministers of the day, and particularly to Sir John Hippisley, who, after three years of persevering and tedious negotiation, had reached so happy a conclusion. They expressed their gratitude, accordingly, in an appropriate letter to Sir John, dated at Edinburgh, June 19th, 1799. Bishop Hay, at the suggestion of Sir John Hippisley, also wrote a letter of thanks, in his own and his colleague's name, to Mr. Secretary Dundas. It was favoured with a prompt and highly complimentary reply :

29th July, 1799.

"REVEREND SIRS—It is with much pleasure, that I acknowledge the receipt of your letter, particularly as I find by it that the aid which his Majesty's Government has been enabled to extend to you and the rest of the Roman Catholic Clergy under your authority, promises to afford so much comfort and relief to to such a pious, loyal and respectable body of men as the Roman Catholic Clergy of Scotland have constantly shown themselves, and which I can have no doubt they will ever continue to be, while they have the benefit of such an example as you have invariably given them. With every good wish for your future health and happiness, I remain with much respect and regard,

"Reverend Sirs,
"Your very faithful, humble servant,
"HENRY DUNDAS."

Another proof of the liberality of our statesmen in the closing days of last century, and which shows also the general decline of bigotry, was presented by an order of the Adjutant-General to the effect that non-commissioned officers and men should be permitted to attend divine worship in the churches, chapels, or meeting houses to which they belong, when an opportunity for their doing so should offer. The Government, to their credit, let it be recorded, lost no opportunity of moderating the wrath of persecuting lairds. A tyrannical proprietor had lodged a groundless accusation against a priest. The Lord Advocate declined to entertain it, and only took occasion to request Bishop Hay to assist him in promoting better feelings between the priest and Laird of Barra.

Now that the French were away from Rome, an army of twenty thousand Neapolitans having driven them from the city, a few months after they had seized it, Mr. Sloane, the devoted friend, as we have seen, of the Scotch College, thought that the time had come for the restoration of the College and its estates. He accordingly addressed Sir William Hamilton at Naples, asking him to use his influence for the recovery of so much British property. It was too soon. But neither Mr. Sloane nor any one else could foresee, at the time, that the French had not yet done with Rome. The Bishops, meanwhile, were making amends for the loss of the Colleges abroad by establishing seminaries at home. The Ministers of the Crown looked with favour on this work of the Bishops. They, as well as all other public men, were agreed as to the importance of encouraging the education of Catholic priests at home, conceiving it to be an essential part of a good education to be made acquainted with the principles of the British Constitution. It was with a view to this great advantage that so much was done in more happy times, especially by Sir John Hippisley, in order to obtain national Superiors for the British Colleges. Sir John now held the opinion that if

Bishop Hay could procure an adequate establishment for ecclesiastical education in Scotland, he would never have cause to regret the loss of the Roman College.

The severe and prolonged sufferings of the invalid Bishop at Aberdeen were now drawing to a close. In the earlier half of January there was an aggravation of his ailments. His back was laid open in two places, by bed sores, which, as he was obliged to lay in one position in bed, were of the worst description. Mortification supervened. Meanwhile the sufferer was a pattern of patience. He never complained of pain. It was frosty weather and the attending physician, Sir Alexander Bannerman, expressed the opinion that, as soon as a thaw set in, the final change would come; and accordingly it came, slowly and surely, like the maladies by which it was preceded. It began on Saturday, February 9th, and was complete, all suffering at an end, the following Monday at five o'clock in the afternoon. The snow churchyard (*Sta. Maria ad Nives*) was chosen for the place of his funeral. There was a large gathering of mourners, including the more notable people of the city. The Professors of King's College University, proprietors of the beautiful cemetery, declined to accept the usual fees. They desired no more than the signal honour that the bones of so great and so good a man were laid at rest within their ground.

Almost all the learned Bishop's printed works including his tract, "*Watch and Pray*," a second edition of which was issued shortly before his death, have been already herein alluded to. He left, besides several manuscripts which are accessible to all who desire seriously to consult them; and will long be held to be a treasure of no ordinary value to the student of history. They are, as follows: 1st, A Catalogue of the Scotch Missionaries; 2nd, A short account of Mr. Ballantyne, first Prefect of the Mission; 3rd, An Account of the Bishop's Journey to Paris in 1791, on the affairs of the Scotch College; 4th, A Letter to the Scotch Agent in Rome on his duties; 5th, Observations relating to the Catholic Missions in Scotland; 6th, A Short Account of the state of Religion in Scotland in 1745-46; 7th, Observations on the duties of a Catholic missionary. It is also said, and on competent authority, that Bishop Geddes was the author of a *Life of Cardinal Innes*, which appeared in the Antiquarian Transactions, about 1794; and was republished in the Edinburgh Monthly Register, June, 1810.

When the Bishops of Scotland were incurring so much expense providing seminaries at home in place of the colleges abroad of which they were deprived, a new calamity came to aggravate their difficulties.

They had been in the habit of receiving, hitherto, substantial aid from the Congregation of Propaganda. This great institution which did so much to maintain the Christian faith in many countries and establish it in others, was now robbed of its properties by the Revolutionists and reduced to poverty. The usual remittance to the Scotch mission could no longer be looked for. This evil, however, was soon repaired through the generosity of a pious and wealthy person in Spain who contributed, yearly, a sum equal to what was expended by Propaganda for the support of the missions and colleges that were confided to its care. The benefactor chose to remain unknown. The news of this liberality gave the greatest joy and consolation to Pius VI., and he thanked God who thus extended protection to His afflicted Church.

The shameful conduct of the French towards the Church and its venerable chief brought no blessings with it. Not only were they driven from Rome. In Upper Italy their army, under Scherer, was beaten by the Austrians and Russians, commanded by Suwarroff. They took Milan and threatened Piedmont. It was soon learned that they had advanced as far as Susa, and it was announced in the Paris Gazette that Suwarroff, Commander of the Imperial armies, had orders to use his utmost efforts for the deliverance of the Pope. The dread of the Holy Father being rescued caused him to be conveyed to Valence, where he died. General Scherer was succeeded in the command of the army of Italy by the celebrated Moreau. Under Scherer began, under Moreau was completed the loss of Bonaparte's conquests. The latter fell back before Suwaroff to the foot of the Alps. He then resigned and was replaced by General Joubert, who fell by a bullet wound at the commencement of the battle in which the French were defeated. The Russians penetrated into the French departments of Mount Blanc and the higher Alps (Hautes Alpes). But they were beaten at Zurich by Massena. Thus were the danger and disquietude of the French Republic diminished, but far from ended.

CAP. LVII.

COMBINATION AGAINST THE FRENCH REVOLUTION—
THE 18TH "BRUMAIRE"—BONAPARTE THE EXE-
CUTIVE POWER—THE ELECTION OF PIUS VII.
FAVOURED BY THE GREAT POWERS — JOYFUL
DEMONSTRATIONS AS HE REPAIRED TO ROME—
RUSSIA'S IMPERIAL SALUTE—HOPES OF THE SCOTCH
BISHOPS — PECUNIARY RELIEF — SEMINARY RE-
MOVED TO AQUORTIES—BISHOP HAY FIRST PRESI-
DENT—HIS PATIENCE IN TEACHING—HIS HABITS.
—USE OF TOBACCO—HIS KINDNESS TO STUDENTS
—STATESMEN RECOMMEND HAVING FEW STUDENTS
TOGETHER—HENCE BISHOP CHISHOLM FOUNDS A
SEMINARY AT LISMORE—EXCELLENT SITE, PRICE
£4,950.

France, stripped of its most brilliant conquests and driven back upon its frontiers, was threatened by a most formidable coalition. Great Britain, Germany, Russia, and even Turkey, provoked by the invasion of Egypt, made common cause with the rest of Europe, against France, and prepared to drive the French from Ancona. The people of Italy, disgusted by the impiety of the French Republicans, their pillage of the Sanctuary of Loretto and the persecution of the Pope, welcomed the Austrians and Russians as liberators. The King of Naples had declared himself in favour of the coalition; and the King of Spain, if he had dared, would have done the same. Suwarroff, who, in 1794, had given the last fatal blow to Poland in order that it might be finally partitioned between Russia, Austria and Prussia, would not have been sorry to give a like fate to revolutionary France. The French Republic, thus threatened from without by Europe in arms, was seriously disturbed interiorly by conspiracies, by Vendeans, Chouans, etc. It was sick at heart, and sick to death. Its failure was a prelude to the most despotic monarchy. Napoleon Bonaparte arrived from his Egyptian exile; and the French Revolution, although it enjoyed for a little while *the name*, was no longer *the thing* called a Republic. The 18th "Brumaire," and Napoleon Bonaparte was the sole executive power with the army at his command. This unlooked for event took the world by surprise. A still more astonishing event was in store—the election of another Pope. After the deportation of Pius VI. and the occupation of Rome and Italy by the French, infidelity, heresy and schism held the opinion, even openly declared, that the Papacy was used up, and Pius VI. would have no successor; and, indeed, what human aid could be counted on? There was not a power that had not shown hostility. All the European powers, meanwhile, including Turkey, had formed a coalition against the revolutionary power of France. Hence, Europe in arms, commanded peace. The conclave assembled at Venice, an Austrian City. The armed powers, not excepting Russia and the sublime Port kept watch at its gates. Peace reigned supreme. Christendom, it is no exaggeration to say, held its breath in expectation of the coming spiritual chief. The Cardinals, undisturbed and without fear of disturbance, proceeded with their usual slowness and deliberation to the election of a Sovereign Pontiff. Several Cardinals were named and well supported; but for want of the requisite number of votes and other causes their candidature did not succeed. Curiously enough, Cardinal Chiaramonti was not thought of till Secretary Consalvi suggested that he should be declared a candidate. To this no Cardinal objected but himself, and a whole fortnight elapsed before his opposition was overcome. This amiable and affectionate dignitary was well known to possess every quality essential to a Pope; and, accordingly, he at once obtained the necessary number of votes, two-thirds of the whole. The rest acceding he was unanimously elected. There was but one opponent, Chiaramonti himself. He could not, however, resist the general will.

The Court of Vienna appeared to be offended by the election of Chiaramonti. They ungraciously refused to let him be crowned in the Church of St. Mark. On the 21st of March, the cermony of crowning took place in the Church of St. George, Cardinal Anthony Doria, Dean of the Cardinals deacon, officiating. The Austrians spoke of retaining the Pope at Venice. They even thought of inducing him to take up his abode at Vienna. When Bonaparte reached the plains of Italy, they no longer opposed the departure of the Pope. He took passage, accordingly, in an Austrian frigate, and landed at Pesaro. He thence journeyed to Rome. He was received at Ancona amid salvos of artillery. The Russian ships stationed at the port, gave an imperial salute according to the orders of their Emperor, Paul I., six hundred Anconians unyoked the horses of his carriage, and, using ropes ornamented with ribbons of different colours, drew it to the palace of the Cardinal Bishop. About eight months before, the Neapolitans, assisted by some Austrian squadrons and two hundred British infantry, drove the French from Rome. They were now displeased at the arrival of the Pope, who entered Rome on the 3rd of June, 1800, the whole people making excessive demonstrations of joy. The Naples Government was obliged to recall from Rome all its troops; but continued to occupy Benevent and Ponte Corvo, which were provinces of the Holy See.

As the Bishops of Scotland had grieved over the deportation of Pius VI., so they now rejoiced on hearing of the advent to Rome of his successor. They hoped, through a continuance of Pius VII.'s prosperity, to derive some benefit from the Roman College, and to obtain the usual aid from Propaganda. Meanwhile their financial difficulties were so far relieved by a timely bequest. Mr. Alexander Menzies, a religious Benedictine of the Pitfodels family, died at Achintoul, where he had been for some time chaplain. He had formerly been a member of the community at Ratisbon. He was much and generally regretted; but by none more than by Bishop Hay, who, having the greatest confidence in his judgment and sincerity, often consulted him. The brethren of Ratisbon were not always conspicuous for their liberality. It was otherwise, however, with Mr. Menzies and Abbot Arbuthnot. Mr. Menzies left a letter to be delivered by Bishop Hay to the Abbot, in which he requested that, at least, half of several hundred pounds which he left behind him, should be given to the fund of the secular mission. He also left a will in which Bishop Hay was named sole executor. The Abbot was to have the offer of all his money. The poor were to have what the sale of his clothes might bring. His books and linen, he requested, might be given to his brother monk, Mr. Robertson. Abbot Arbuthnot, in compliance with the deceased brother's last wishes, and also from a spirit of liberality, for it was fully in his power to do otherwise, consented to a division of Mr. Menzies' money between the monastery and the mission. The half amounted to something more than £400.

In July, 1799, the seminary was removed from Scalan to Aquorties. The Bishop himself was the first president at the new house, which, at first, could maintain only six students although there was room for thirty, so great had been the expense of preparing the building. This inconvenience was only temporary, and in course of some time the seminary had its full complement of thirty pupils, with a suitable staff of professors and servants. It cost the Bishop a great deal to leave Scalan, to which he was much attached. It grieved him also to part with the good people of the neighbourhood. The very remoteness and solitude of Scalan had a charm for him. The cultivated and fertile fields around it with its picturesque mountain scenery must be exchanged for the bleak and dreary morass of Aquorties; for, it was not then what it has since become, a beautiful and smiling farm. The charge of a few boys and the tedious labour incident thereto, must have been a serious trial to a man of Bishop Hay's active habits, who had been so long accustomed to the best social intercourse and intimate relations with the distinguished men of the capital. But he had at heart the founding of an important educational institution and the sacrifice must be made. It was found that the actual cost of the buildings greatly exceeded the estimate. Hence, it came to be necessary that every shilling of his own which he could spare should be called for, before even a commencement could be made. It was not enough for the Bishop to superintend. He also took his share in the daily work, as long as he was able. He taught the classes of mental philosophy and metaphysics, using as his text book Dr. Reid's Works on the Moral and Intellectual Powers. Besides lecturing on those subjects, which he studied to explain with as much clearness as they admitted of, the Bishop has left behind him a monument of his patient and humble industry in a mass of manuscript abridgments from many authors, for the use of his pupils, both at Scalan and Aquorties. It was probably as a relaxation from his more abstruse studies that he taught the rudiments of grammar, and was so fond of this work that he had a class of little boys engaged in it. He took pleasure in being with the students. He went to breakfast, dinner and supper with them in the refectory, and never failed to attend the evening prayers of the community in the chapel, and other religious exercises. All this did not hinder him from devoting several hours of the day to mental prayer and spiritual reading, sometimes in the chapel, sometimes in his room, and pretty often, out of doors. He celebrated Mass every morning, except when the state of his health required that he should take some refection at an early hour, or, perhaps, a little medicine.

The reader may, at first, be shocked when told that a Bishop of unquestioned holiness of life, indulged in the ugly habit of chewing tobacco. But let him have patience. One day the student who acted as sacristan (afterdwards well known as the Rev. Mr. Carmichael), asked the Bishop how he came to acquire such a habit. He had no hesitation in satisfying the young man's curiosity. "Do you think that for any cause I would continue that nasty habit if I did not find it necessary? I will tell you the reason. I was long subject to a state of health which occasioned me violent headaches, and I tried every remedy I could think of to no purpose till I tried the daily use of small twist which keeps me in a much more healthy condition. Were I to give up chewing tobacco my old complaints and their bad effects would follow; I am, therefore, to continue the ugly practice." Most drugs are unpleasant, but the patient who loves health more than he hates physic will, nevertheless gladly swallow them.

The Bishop was much with the students in recreation hours. They listened with delight to the many stories he could tell relating to bygone times. He thus amused, and, in amusing, instructed them. He often spent the winter evenings among them when they played the Italian game of "cuckoos," distributed prizes and otherwise contributed to their amusements.

When any of the boys were sick, the Bishop, who had not forgot his medical learning, not only prescribed for them, but also administered medicines to them with his own hands. In the case of their being confined to bed, he often remained in the room with them, saying his prayers and helping them by turns, with the tenderness of a nurse, till he saw they were better.

It had been in contemplation to erect a College on a large scale for both districts. The Government, however, was opposed to the scheme. So much ill-will, prejudice, jealousy and rancour still prevailed among the lower class of people towards Catholics, that there might be dangerous consequences if many students were assembled in one place. The Lord

Advocate, therefore advised the Bishop to begin his seminary with a few pupils, and afterwards increase their numbers when circumstances warranted a change. This wise advice was not lost on the Bishops; and Bishop Chisholm immediately set about establishing a seminary for the Highland district. The Island of Lismore was the locality selected by the Bishop. There was on this island a suitable site which could be purchased. The proprietor, Campbell, of Dunstaffnage, had erected on it a substantial house some years before. There was also an excellent garden. The land was good and limestone abundant. It was the opinion in Edinburgh that the purchase would be an advantageous one at the price demanded, £4,950. It was of easy access from Glasgow, which gave it additional advantages as regarded the conveyance of coal and other things necessary for the use of the establishment. Among the many attractions of the place there was one which could not fail to interest a Catholic purchaser. It had been the residence of the Bishop of Argyle.

CAP. LVIII.

GOVERNMENT GRANT—DELAY—SIR JOHN HIPPISLEY SUCCESSFUL—COLLEGE PROPERTY AT ROME—MR. ANDREW SCOTT AT HUNTLEY—THE LIVES OF THE SAINTS—DEMAND FOR RELIGIOUS BOOKS—NEED OF A LARGE CHURCH AT EDINBURGH—DIFFICULTIES—ELECTION OF PIUS VII.—THE BISHOPS OFFICIALLY INFORMED — CONGRATULATIONS — SCOTCH PROPERTY AT ROME—CLAIMED FROM THE NEAPOLITAN GENERAL—ITS DESPERATE CONDITION —APPEAL TO BRITISH GOVERNMENT—LETTERS TO ROME—THE CLERGY PETITION FOR ADDITIONAL INCOME.

There was difficulty and delay in obtaining payment of the money granted by Government for the benefit of the Catholic clergy in Scotland. Sir John Hippisley was, on application, informed that the Secretary of the Treasury had recieved orders to intimate to the Lord Advocate that the money would be paid in three weeks from the date of Sir John's letter (August 27th, 1799). Nine weeks elapsed when Sir John went to the Treasury and was told that there was a difficulty, the Scotch Catholic clergy having no representative in London. On hearing this, Sir John immediately wrote to Bishop Hay, requesting that he would lose no time in sending a power of attorney in his own name and that of Bishop Chisholm, authorizing him (Sir John) and Mr. Spalding, M. P. for the Galloway Burghs, to receive the money granted to the Scotch clergy. There was only a weekly mail to the nearest town from Moydart, where Bishop Chisholm was staying at his seminary. This remoteness of the Highland Bishop was the cause of further delay, but not the end of it. Sir John on presenting the power of attorney, was informed that there was so great a run on the treasury that the payment he desired could not be made sooner than shortly before Christmas.

It proved however to be a good deal later. Only on the 21st January, 1800, was the Procurator able to acquaint Bishop Hay that the money for the mission was paid. Much it may be said, all, in this matter, was due to the determined perseverance of Sir John Hippisley.

There was now some hope of recovering the College property in Rome, and it was decided that Mr. McPherson should resume his duties as agent. This re-appointment to his former office at Rome was much to his liking; and a commission was prepared, in the name of both the Bishops, empowering him to act for them in recovering the property of the mission in Italy. He was replaced in the mission of Huntly by Mr. Andrew Scott, who was afterwards so highly distinguished. Mr. Moir, a British resident in Rome, was empowered to act in the interest of the mission till the arrival of the agent.

The reprinting of the Lives of the Saints now commenced was quite an undertaking. There appears to have been, at the time, a demand for religious publications. Bishop Hay's three best known works were out of print.

The Catholics of Edinburgh conceived the idea of having one large church, in which both congregations could meet, instead of the two small chapels in Blackfriar's Wynd. Mr. C. Maxwell, their pastor, was at the head of the movement; and proposed to purchase a house in the Canongate, which, according to his description, was very eligible for the priest's residence, while the garden attached to it, a quarter of an acre in extent, presented a suitable site for the new church. It had been the city mansion of the Earl of Wemyss, by whom it was built. The price demanded was 1,000 guineas. The Bishop could not see any reason for encouraging the scheme. He told Mr. Maxwell that no dependence could be placed on subscriptions from the Catholice in the north. They had already aided in building chapels all over the country and were quite unprepared for any new call on their charity. As to the Bishop himself. owing to the many demands upon him, he was unable to give any assistance. All that he could do was to authorize the sale of the two old chapels in aid of the new building.

This, however, could not be done until the proposed chapel was ready for use. Mr. Maxwell could have no assurance that the inhabitants in the neighbourhood of the intended site would not object to and oppose the erection of a Catholic chapel after the Catholics were committed to it by the purchase of the house. There was powerful opposition to have St. Margaret's chapel in the house that was purchased for it. The Bishop was met with a lawsuit, which, however, was decided, fortunately in his favour. If the project continued to be entertained, the Bishop would have Mr. Maxwell break the matter to the Lord Advocate and the Lord Provost, in order to learn their opinion. He desired, moreover, to hear what was said against the scheme, and particularly by the Rev. Mr. Rattray, on whose judgment he placed great reliance. Mr. Rattray vigourously opposed the measure; and, first of all because a chapel in the Canongate would not be convenient for the congregation. In the second place, the house was too small for the residence of the clergy. It was only a wing of the house built by Lord Wemyss about 1735. The actual proprietor, a bookseller, had bought it a few years previously, for £350, and the value of houses in that part of the town had been falling ever since, the proprietors generally being glad to sell them at any price, and remove to the more fashionable new town. Notwithstanding all this, the wily bookseller had deceived Mr. Maxwell and persuaded him to offer £1,000 for the remaining part of Lord Wemyss' residence. Mr. Maxwell was indignant at Mr. Rattray's interference; and it was not without difficulty that the latter succeeded in preventing a bargain from being concluded until the Bishop could be heard from. The Bishop, with his usual caution, declined to give a decision until he had learned everything connected with the proposed scheme. He accordingly authorized Mr. Rattray to obtain from the committee that was entrusted with the care of promoting the plan of the new chapel, an exact description of the building which it was proposed to purchase, signed by every member of the committee, together with all other particulars that were calculated to throw light on the subject. Financial difficulties were also taken into consideration; and finally, the idea of purchasing for £1,000 a house for which the proprietor had paid only £350, was abandoned. It was reserved for Bishop Hay's distinguished successor to erect a large and more handsome church in a suitable part of the city. While the discussion regarding the proposed new chapel was proceeding, the Bishop received official information from Cardinal Erskine of the election of Pope Pius VII. He immediately imparted the same to Bishop Chisholm, as well as to the clergy of his own district. It now became the duty of the Bishop to compliment the Holy Father on his accession to the Chair of Peter. He had never failed to fulfil this duty on former occasions; and he now only waited for the concurrence of his colleague, Bishop Chisholm. It was decided, accordingly, that when the Bishops met in July they should send to Rome a joint letter of congratulation. In the meantime, Bishop Hay acquainted Cardinal Erskine with the wise intention.

The Neapolitans having taken Rome, it was now thought that something might be done towards the recovery of the Scotch property there. Mr. Moir, who held a letter of procuration authorizing him to deal with this property, found that he was anticipated by a Mr. Fagan. This person, as soon as the city was occupied by the army of Naples, claimed restitution of all British property from the Neapolitan General. Mr. Moir, on this account, found it necessary to use his letter of procuration, but declined doing anything until the arrival of Mr. McPherson.

This gentleman reached the city in July, 1800. He found the Scotch College and its property in a deplorable condition. "The house," he says, writing to Bishop Hay, "is going fast to ruin. It is let out to almost as many different families as there are rooms in it, all wretchedly poor creatures, unable to pay the rent, or keep the house in repair. I wished Mr. Fagan to turn them out. He attempted to do so, and could have done it at pleasure, a month or two back. But, ever since Cardinal Albani returned to Rome, they have got protectors enough among his creatures, and laugh at Fagan. I have seen the Cardinal. He says till Fagan resigns all his assumed power, he will do nothing. His minions do enough. In the meantime, I am obliged to take up my quarters elsewhere, and if ever I get into the College it will now be with difficulty and not on the terms you and I expected. The old rector is returned and has by far more interest in Albani's court than I. The vineyards, already in a wretched state, will be in a worse one before we have anything to do with them. They have been let by Mr. Fagan till the end of this year, for one hundred and a few odd crowns. Hence, till autumn of 1801, though I get possession the College, I cannot touch a half-penny of the revenues. But, to me it appears very improbable I will get possession of it." (11th July, 1800.)

In the same letter Mr. McPherson suggested that application should be made, through Mr. George Chalmers, who had always shown himself very friendly, to the British Ministry, asking them to use their influence with the Neapolitan Government, for complete restoration to its rightful owners of the Scotch College and the property attached to it.

Bishop Chisholm came in July to meet his colleague at Aquorties; and there the two Bishops prepared their annual letters,—one in Latin to the new Pope, and another in Italian, to Cardinal Borgia, Pro Prefect of Propaganda. These they enclosed in a complimentary letter to Monsignor Erskine. The routine of the annual meeting was diversified by the presentation of a petition to Bishop Hay by some of the clergy of his district, which could only be justified by the difficulties to which they were subjected in consequence of the scantiness of their incomes. It requested that the Bishop would both urgently and speedily use his influence with their congregations to induce them to raise their annual allowance to £50. This does not appear to be an extravagant request, unless, indeed, the purchasing power of money was much greater at that time than it is now. The petition was adopted at a meeting of the clergy held at Preshome, the preceding month of May. It was presented by Messrs. Stuart and Scott on the part of their brethren. There was nothing unreasonable in the petition, as may be judged from the names that were appended to it, such as Mr. Paterson, afterwards Bishop at Edinburgh, Mr. Mathieson, Mr. John Reid, Mr. George Gordon (late of Dufftown), Mr. James Carruthers and Mr. James Sharp. These clergymen were all highly esteemed by the Bishop. Their petition was, however, considered unreasonable since it was necessary to obtain a Government grant in order to provide for existing charges, and when the people were in a distressed condition, from the scarcity of provisions. Bishop Hay received it respectfully, but, finally, could not see grounds for entertaining it. In stating his reasons for declining, the Bishop incidentally mentioned that thirty years before. the mission funds in the whole of Scotland, did not exceed £60 a year. The accounts of 1769 show a home revenue of only £48 belonging to the mission. Its foreign income was £200, with twenty-four missionaries to share it, while, owing to the exertions of the Bishop (which was chiefly Bishop Hay's), they produced at the date of the meeting of 1800, a yearly income of £466, which was equal to a capital of more than £8,000.

CAP. LIX.

THE BRITISH COLLEGES AT ROME—THE NEW SEMINARY IN SCOTLAND SOLIDLY ESTABLISHED—THE BISHOP OF THE HIGHLAND DISTRICT PURCHASES AN ELIGIBLE SITE FOR A COLLEGE IN THE ISLAND OF LISMORE, PRICE £4,950—THE HIGHEST STATESMEN FAVOUR CATHOLIC EMANCIPATION—THE CORONATION OATH AN IMPEDIMENT—SALARIES OF THE CLERGY—A FALSE ACCUSATION—VOTE OF CONFIDENCE IN THE BISHOP—THE BISHOP DETERMINES ON PRESERVING THE SCOTCH COLLEGE AT ROME—GRATITUDE TO THE GOVERNMENT, HONOUR AND LOYALTY TO THE KING—OBJECTIONS TO THE CLERGY ACTING POLITICALLY—THE SCOTCH COLLEGE AT PARIS—LARGER CHURCH NEEDED AT EDINBURGH—THE LORD ADVOCATE FAVOURABLE—SUBSCRIPTIONS—SITE—VANDYKE'S "DESCENT FROM THE CROSS"—BISHOP CAMERON'S RETURN—WHY DELAYED—MR. ANDREW CARRUTHERS AND CERTAIN REGULATIONS.

Pius VII. had no sooner arrived in Rome than negotiations were recommenced with a view to have national superiors placed over the British and Irish Colleges. The agent was powerless. All the high dignitaries were against him, with the exception of Cardinal York and the Secretary of Propaganda, Monsignor Brancadoro. They mistrusted the agent as an intruder on the exclusive privilege of the Italians. Opposed to their views was, it may be said, the whole power of the British Government, through the indefatigable exertions of Sir John Hippisley. This able and friendly diplomatist addressed letters on the subject to many of the Cardinals and even to the Pope himself. In doing so he had the full support of the influence and authority of the British Government. At the same time all the British and Irish Catholic Bishops united in presenting a memorial to His Holiness praying for the restoration of the National Colleges in Rome, and that they should be placed on such a footing as to compensate in some degree, for the losses sustained in France. They prayed also that national superiors should be appointed over the Colleges.

The labours of the Bishop were at this time very severe, and the more so as he enjoyed not as yet the assistance of his recently appointed coadjutor. He was indefatigable in his visitations; and the interest he took in the new seminary imposed on him additional care and work that would have afforded more than sufficient employment for his undivided energies. The low state of the College funds, consequent upon its transference to Aquorties, and the erection of a new building, added not a little to his cares. It could not yet compare with the ancient institutions of the continent; but it was established on a safe and solid basis, and destined in due time to produce abundant fruit.

1781. The Bishop of the Highland district now set about accomplishing the purpose which the Bishops had intimated to Propaganda. The Island of Lismore was selected for a site. The proprietor, Campbell, of Dunstaffnage, a few years before had built on the island a substantial house, attached to which there was an excellent garden. The land was good, and there was abundance of limestone. It was the opinion in Edinburgh that it was a good purchase at the price required, £4,950. It was very accesible from the great commercial city of Glasgow, a circumstance which gave it great facilities for the conveyance of coal and such other things as were necessary for the use of the seminary. It was an additional recommendation that it had once been the residence of the Bishop of Argyle.

The services and influence of Sir John Hippisley had been mainly instrumental in obtaining a grant of money to the mission from the Government. He now renewed negotiations for obtaining a remittance of this grant, and was favoured with the promise that a payment of £1,600 would be made within forty days. About the same time this active and friendly public man informed Mr. McPherson that the British Cabinet was divided on the subject of Catholic Emancipation. Mr. Pitt, Lord Spencer, Lord Grenville, Mr. Dundas and Mr. Wyndham were in favour of granting the boon, and in consequence resigned. King George III. had scruples in regard to his Coronation Oath which could not be overcome. All arguments he treated as incomprehensible metaphysics. Such, at least, was Mr. Dundas' experience of the royal mind. When pressed by this Minister, with cogent reasoning, he told the great statesman that *he would have none of his Scotch metaphysics.*

The clergy, this year, renewed their application for an increase of salary, insisting that the Bishop should lay upon their congregations the obligation of contributing towards their support. This request was met by a determined refusal, the Bishop holding that such contributing ought to be left to the free will of the people. The influence of the pastors with their flocks, one would suppose, might have prevailed so far as to induce them to add something to salaries that were so small and insufficient. The clergy, nevertheless, persisted clamourously in their representations to the Bishop, and even went so far as to accuse him of appropriating the money granted by

Government to his own use and that of his seminary. They were encouraged in this idea by the knowledge that each student in his new College cost him £27 a year. The procurator, Mr. C. Maxwell, who knew all the details, concurred with the Bishop in stating that the money in question had been properly distributed. This statement, coming as it did, from *the head of the opposition*, ought to have satisfied the malcontents. In this matter, however, the procurator could not oppose the Bishop, as, owing to the duties of his office he was perfectly conversant with the facts of the case. A few of the clergy, notwithstanding, on whom their poverty pressed heavily in a season of scarcity, would not take his word, and continued in their course. The Bishop, hitherto, had not made sufficient account of public opinion, which, if rightly informed, would have supported him. A full statement of the distribution of the funds was laid before a meeting of the administrators and a deputation of the discontented clergy at Aberdeen. With this statement all were satisfied, as they could not fail to be. There only remained the humiliation of the Bishop being judged by his subordinates; and this might have been avoided if, in deference to opinion, he had made an earlier statement as to how, through the procurator, the funds in question had been disposed of. The scheme of division originated with the Government; and it behoved the Bishops to carry it out. A unanimous vote of confidence was passed in Bishop Hay's honour and integrity, and recorded in the minutes of the meeting. It was declared, moreover, that all past complaints against him were nothing better than vague and unfounded assertions, deserving only to be totally disregarded.

At this time (1801) the Scotch College at Rome was deeply in debt; and, as the mission at home was unable to do anything towards relieving it, the only way of removing the liabilities appeared to be to sell the College properties. To this plan, however, the Bishop was opposed so long as there remained a chance of retrieving its fortunes.

At a meeting of administrators held this year, inquiry was made as to the precise nature of the transactions with Government, and the proceedings were appropriately terminated with a letter of thanks addressed by the meeting to Sir John Hippisley as the sincere and disinterested friend and benefactor of the mission. It was requested in the letter, that, as a new favour, Sir John would assure His Majesty's Ministers of the heartfelt gratitude of the Scotch clergy for the late act of benevolence; and of their habitual disposition to cultivate in their own minds, and to propagate among their people sentiments of loyalty to His Majesty's sacred person, and of attachment to the happy Constitution under which they lived. Sir John lost no time in returning a suitable reply to this complimentary and loyal address.

A contest for the representation of Aberdeenshire being near at hand, it was not unreasonable that Sir John should look to the Scotch Bishop for some return of the favours which the Government had so liberally bestowed. Mr. Ferguson, the Government candidate, had warmly seconded Sir John's appeal to Mr. Dundas for a grant to the clergy, and had borne ample testimony to the loyalty of the Catholics in his neighbourhood. None knew better than Sir John Hippisley that the Catholic clergy could not prudently take an active part in a contested election; but if Bishop Hay could fall upon some means that would not be open to any reasonable objection, of promoting Mr. Ferguson's candidature, it would be a favour to himself as well as to the Government.

The Bishops held their annual meeting this year at Aberdeen. The affairs of the Scotch College in France engaged their attention. As there was a prospect of peace, they were encouraged to hope for the recovery of, at least, a part of the mission property. Sir John Hippisley readily took part in the necessary negotiations. The Bishop memorialized the Foreign Secretary, Lord Hawkesbury, requesting him to promote the realizing and withdrawing from France all the property of the mission, both at Paris and at Douai ; and the transference of it to Scotland. Meanwhile, the ex-Principal, Mr. Gordon, had returned to Paris and did everything in his power to thwart Mr. Innes, who acted for the mission. Such proceeding greatly increased the difficulty of negotiations, which, even without this hindrance, were not of the most facile description. Bishop Hay was obliged to journey to Edinburgh in November, in order to take counsel with Mr. Maxwell and Mr. Farquarson on the subject. The result of this consultation was that Mr. Innes received full power to represent the interests of the mission and to act for the Scotch Bishops. Finally, Mr. Farquarson was sent to Paris in order to assist him.

At this time there was a great desire among the Catholics to have a larger and more handsome church at Edinburgh. The scheme of Mr. C. Maxwell having been discarded as impracticable, Mr. Rattray conceived a design less open to objection. He began by conciliating the good will of the chief public men. He addressed the new Lord Advocate, Mr. Hope, intimating the proposal, and requesting his concurrence. The ex-Lord Advocate, now Chief Baron of Exchequer, was also consulted and asked to concur. Mr. Hope, on his own part and that of his predecessor, with much politeness, declined to offer any opposition to the proposed plan; but reminded Mr. Rattray of the strong prejudice that still existed in the country against his form of religion, and, therefore, advised him to do nothing that might excite it. The more quietly the matter could be managed the better; and the subscription ought not to be publicly advertised. He himself, as a member of the Established Church, regretted that weak brethren might consider it an impropriety if the subscription opened with his name. He promised, however, to protect any of the Catholics who might, in future, be exposed to the illegal opposition or the insults of misguided people. Mr. Rattray having thus far provided against opposition at home, set about securing funds for the proposed undertaking. His chief hope lay in the English Catholic body, although, at the same time, the aid of his Scotch friends was not to be despised. Mr. Marmaduke Maxwell, of Terreagles, was among the first to place his name on the subscription list, and for the munificent sum of 100 guineas. Mr. Weld, of Lulworth, also co-operated; and, finding that "good Bishop Hay" was still in life, begged Mr. Rattray to assure him of his veneration and esteem for him. The distinguished banker, Sir William Forbes, who was the chief pillar of the Episcopalian body, gave his name for £10. Early in the year 1802 the subscriptions amounted to

£900. Among the subscribers were the Duchess of Buccleugh, Lord Moira and other Protestants. Not a little of this liberality was due to the memory of Bishop Geddes, most of the contributors being among his personal friends. As was to be expected, Dr. Alexander Wood, Bishop Hay's old and devoted friend, subscribed. Mr. Rattray was eminently successful among all classes; so much so that he thought little of an English Catholic nobleman's subscription of £5, although it was accompanied by a promise to solicit other subscriptions. As the subscriptions were proceeding, a site for a church and house adjoining was purchased between St. James' Square and York place. It measured one hundred and twelve feet by forty-five. The price was over £300. The time for building, however, had not yet arrived; nor was the purchased site finally accepted. It behoved it to give place to another in the same neighbourhood which was in every way more convenient, and on which the pro-Cathedral now stands. A painting by Vandyke, representing the "Descent from the Cross," was the altar piece, and still remains so in the more recent church, if no better has been found, having survived all dangers.

Although Mr. Farquarson remained at Paris till June, he did not succeed in accomplishing anything. He was anxious to regain his congregation in Glasgow, which, during his absence, was without a pastor. Bishop Cameron joined him late in May, on his return from Valladolid, where he had officiated for some time as Bishop, and they travelled home in company. The new Bishop enjoyed great favour, and had many friends in Spain; so it is not surprising that the whole city of Valladolid regretted his departure, which was considered as a serious loss. A false rumour ascribed to him the ambitious purpose of delaying his return to Scotland until he could rule the district alone. There was nothing farther from his mind, and his arrival, after much hindrance, relieved Bishop Hay of great difficulty and labour, which he was no longer able to undergo. The real causes of the coadjutor's delay were very different from what rumour had laid to his charge. All the time of the war, the Spanish Minister refused to give him a passport. He was detained eighteen months by severe illness. For some time he was without money for his journey, the income of the College having been greatly diminished. The state of the College, also, which stood so much in need of improvement, required his presence; and this necessity induced him to yield to the representations of his friends and advisers at Valladolid, who concurred in detaining him. He left the College in an improved condition. Mr. Wallace remained there as one of the masters, together with Mr. Gordon and Mr. Cameron, the new Bishop's nephew.

There occurred about this time a curious instance of a priest requesting the Bishop to give him information regarding matters of quite a rudimentary kind. This priest was no other than Mr. Andrew Carruthers, the chaplain at Munshes, at the time still a young man. For an answer to the first three of his queries, the Bishop referred him to the *Statutia Missionis*, remarking that however well his correspondent might have studied, he had overlooked hitherto the manual of his daily duties. For the solution of another difficulty, Mr. Carruthers was advised to study a certain chapter and section of the *Sincere Christian*, a work which could scarcely have escaped the notice of any priest in Scotland. There was only one point of general interest, and one of which little could be learned from books. There appears to have prevailed in Galloway at that time, the custom of abstaining from eggs on Ash Wednesday and Good Friday. The Bishop, when he first came to the mission, understood from his predecessors that all *lacticinea*, or, white meats, were used in Lent as common food, and for the very satisfactory reason that by far the greater number of the Catholics in Scotland had no other kind of food at that season of the year. The long winter and late spring deprived them of vegetables; and milk, even, was often scarce when Lent began early. The Bishop found, however, that eggs were not universally used in Lent. All the churches and chapelries which, in Catholic times, were included in the Archiepiscopal Province of St. Andrews, by virtue of an ancient privilege, handed down by constant tradition, made use of eggs from the second Sunday in Lent till Palm Sunday. During the first ten days of Lent and Holy Week they abstained from eggs. The other Scotch parishes, not in the Province of St. Andrews, abstained from eggs during the whole of Lent. Hence, the parish of Bellie, in the Enzie, enjoyed the privilege, while the neighbouring parish of Rathven was denied it. Thus, too, at Aberdeen, eggs were not used in Lent, but were in the Mearns, south of the river Dee. It was also known to the Bishop that, in some inland places, far from the sea, especially in the Highlands, where the winters were longer and the springs later, it had become a custom to use eggs during Lent, except in the first and last weeks.

CAP. LX.

BISHOP CAMERON AS COADJUTOR—BISHOP HAY'S LOAN WITHOUT INTEREST TO THE NEW CHURCH OF ABERDEEN—DEATH OF REV. GEO. MAXWELL, S. J., AT THE AGE OF NINETY—HIS GIFT OF £400 TO STONEYHURST—LIBERAL ALSO TOWARDS THE SEMINARIES OF SCOTLAND — RELIQUES ; A SILVER THURIBLE AND REMONSTRANCE OF HOLYROOD—BISHOP CAMERON AT EDINBURGH; HAS SOLE CHARGE OF THE COUNTRY SOUTH OF THE GRAMPIANS—BISHOP HAY TRANSFERS THE MISSION PROPERTY HELD IN HIS NAME TO TRUSTEES—BISHOP CHISHOLM TAKES POSSESSION OF HIS SEMINARY IN THE ISLAND OF LISMORE—MEETS BISHOPS HAY AND CAMERON AT AQUORTIES—MGR. ERSKINE CARDINAL—BECOMES CARDINAL PROTECTOR—WAR BETWEEN FRANCE AND GREAT BRITAIN—PASTORAL IN SUPPORT OF GOVERNMENT—NEW PRAYER FOR THE KING—BISHOP CAMERON AND THE SPANISH EMBASSY—CHIEF DUTY ON THE COADJUTOR—MR. ÆNEAS CHISHOLM CHOSEN BISHOP OF HIGHLAND DISTRICT—BISHOP MILNER—HOW BISHOP CAMERON TRAVELLED—REPORT TO ROME FROM THE HIGHLANDS—MR. ÆNEAS CHISHOLM'S CONSECRATION.

DELAYED—THE "DEVOUT" AND "PIOUS CHRISTIAN" TRANSLATED INTO FRENCH—THE AUTHOR'S AUTOBIOGRAPHY—BISHOP HAY STRUCK WITH PARALYSIS—RALLIES—REMITTANCE OF 200 CROWNS AND CONGRATULATIONS TO THE SCOTCH BISHOPS.

We now find Bishop Cameron acting for the first time as coadjutor. In August, 1802, he met the Bishops of both districts at Edinburgh, and transacted together with them the usual business of the annual meeting. In the letter to Propaganda it was mentioned that Bishop Hay's memory had failed so much more as to leave him often without words to express his meaning. After the meeting he began his journey back to Aquorties in company with Bishop Cameron. The latter spent a month among his friends in the North, and then returned to Edinburgh for the winter.

A new and better church was now provided at Aberdeen, Mr. Gordon having zealously exerted himself in obtaining subscriptions among his friends. Bishop Hay contributed in the form of a loan of £300 without interest.

It would be a serious omission not to record the death, at ninety years of age, of a venerable priest who had long and faithfully served the mission. This was none other than the ex-Jesuit, Mr. George Maxwell. There was no other disease than the decay incident to old age. His servant found him one day in his chair in a state of stupour. Mr. C. Maxwell hastened to his assistance, and at once administered Extreme Unction and the last blessing. Immediately after this he departed to his rest. Mr. Maxwell was a liberal contributor to the Seminary which his former brethren of the suppressed Order established at Stoneyhurst. His offering was £400 in gold. Notwithstanding some difference of opinion as to the property of the ex-Jesuits in Scotland, there was always a warm friendship between him and Bishop Hay, who highly esteemed him and often consulted him. He bequeathed his money, with the exception of the sum already mentioned, to his Order in the event of it being restored, and the interest thereof, in the meantime, to the Seminaries of Scotland. In connection with Mr. Maxwell's will, the Bishop found it necessary to visit Edinburgh. On his return to Aquorties he wrote a long letter to his coadjutor in which he complains of his fast declining health which was greatly impaired by his recent journey. In the same letter he refers to a relic of the by-gone time—a silver thurible with incense boat attached, together with a Remonstrance or *Soleil* for the exposition of the Blessed Sacrament. These all belonged of old to the Royal Chapel of Holyrood Palace, when the Duke of York, afterwards James VII. and II., held his Court there. The Bishop's friend, M. L'Abbe Latil, desired to have these things as a loan for the use of his small congregation, and they were kindly sent to him.

It does not appear that there was any want of cordiality between the Bishop and his coadjutor. The former certainly could not have given to the latter a warmer or more friendly welcome. The junior Bishop was now to reside at Edinburgh, a fitting place for the commencement of a career that was destined to be so bright. He was also entrusted with the sole charge of the country south of the Grampian Mountains.

The chapel at Aberdeen was now so much enlarged that it might well be termed a church. In our day it would have this designation.

Bishop Hay was now relieved of his more onerous duties, the coadjutor, according to the arrangement entered into, having taken up his residence at Edinburgh. The congregation there was not destined as yet to have a new and more commodious church.

The want of sufficient funds obliged Mr. Rattray to abandon his favourite scheme. The estimated cost, £4000, was beyond any that he had been able to collect. Meanwhile, Bishop Hay was devoting his time and his purse at Aquorties to the improvements of the Seminary. "I am now," he said, writing to Bishop Chisholm, "In a manner, out of the world, and with good reason, for, I am almost good for nothing." He was resolved, however, to do one good thing, and that was to transfer his property and the mission funds that were held in his name, to trustees, in order to avoid the uncertainty and expense of disposing of it by will. The legacy duty alone at the time, a recent invention of financiers, was no inconsiderable item; litigation, which is always costly, might also have jeopardized the funds.

Bishop Chisholm, before repairing to the annual meeting, took possession of his Seminary at Lismore. He then passed over the Grampain Mountains to Aquorties, where Bishops Hay and Cameron awaited him. The annual letters were prepared on the first of August. One of these was a complimentary letter to Mgr. Erskine on occasion of his elevation to the dignity of Cardinal. This Prelate succeeded Cardinal Albani, a few months later, as Cardinal Protector of Scotland. Propaganda had also a new Prefect in succession to Cardinal Borgia. He learned from the Bishop's annual letter to Propaganda the unwelcome fact that Bishop Hay's memory had so much failed that he could no longer attempt to preach or say Mass in public. War had broken out anew between France and Great Britain and became the occasion of a joint pastoral letter which the Bishops issued before closing the meeting. In this letter the people were earnestly called upon to support the Government to the best of their ability, whether by enlisting for military service or by their prayers. The letter was accompanied by a new prayer for the King and Royal Family.

A circumstance now occurred which caused much concern and alarm to Bishop Hay. He dreaded lest he should be deprived of the aid of his coadjutor. Through the Abbe Latil, Chaplain to the exiled Royal Family of France, Bishop Cameron was offered the first chaplaincy of the Spanish Embassy in London. Of the five Spanish chaplains already in office, not one knew a word of the Spanish language. In consequence of this rather singular circumstance, Bishop Cameron, if he had accepted office, must have resided constantly in London. It does not appear that he ever entertained the idea of accepting. But a charge so incompatible with the exercise of his episcopal duties in Scotland was at once rejected.

Bishop Hay's growing infirmities induced him once more to solicit from the authorities at Rome permission to transfer the duties of his office to his coadjutor. In writing to Cardinal Borgia on the subject he gave such an account of his health as appeared to secure a favourable answer to his request. For two years he had not been able to say Mass in public. It was three years since he had preached, so great was the failure of his memory. The most familiar words escaped him, even in conversation. This made him adverse to visiting. He could hardly stand sometimes from attacks of giddiness and great weakness. He was not himself surprised at all this, as he had reached the seventy-fourth year of his age, and the forty-fourth of his missionary labours. The administration of the district besides could not be in more able hands than those of his coadjutor.

New complications now occurred in the affairs of the Scotch College at Paris, in consequence of the death of Mr. Innes; and there was less prospect than ever of recovering the property in France.

Meanwhile, Cardinal Borgia consulted Bishop Hay as to the qualifications of the three candidates named for the coadjutorship of the Highland district. Mr. Æneas Chisholm, a brother of the Bishop, was finally chosen. Soon after another letter from Rome conveyed to Bishop Hay a polite refusal of his request. It may be said, however, to have been virtually granted, as, in the same letter he was advised to lay the chief burden of duty on his coadjutor, but still to retain in his own hands the office of Vicar Apostolic.

The Right Rev. Dr. Milner, so celebrated in the history of the English Church, in a letter to Bishop

Cameron, expressed the hope that "the venerable Bishop Hay was in good health," adding that he had the honour to be known to him twenty-five years ago, when he was in London.

Rumours had got afloat to the effect that the Society of Jesus was re-established, and that Mr. John Pepper had renewed his vows at Stoneyhurst. Bishop Douglas, however, forwarded to Scotland a circular letter from Propaganda which conveyed the information that all such rumours regarding the restoration of the Society, were unfounded; but that they were still limited to the Russian Empire.

We now find the Bishops preparing for the annual meeting. Bishop Cameron resolved to perform a part of the journey from Edinburgh on horseback. For this purpose he purchased a horse at Perth; but a friend insisted on his accepting the loan of a gig in which he travelled by Bræmar, Strathdown, Glenlivat and Huntley to the Seminary at Aquorties. From thence he conveyed Bishop Hay along with him in this easy kind of carriage to Preshome, where the meeting of Bishops took place this year in the middle of August. It was resolved that Mr. John Reid, who had served the mission of Preshome during forty years, should be allowed to retire with an annuity of £50. The Bishops addressed a joint letter of congratulation to Cardinal Erskine on occasion of his succeeding to the Protectorship of the Scotch mission. Detailed replies were prepared to a number of questions regarding the statistics of both districts, addressed by Propaganda to the Bishops. It was the first time any report was ever presented by the Bishop of the Highlands.

At the meeting of administrators, Bishop Hay was induced by his inability to remember words to resign the Presidency to his colleague, Bishop Chisholm. When there was question of anything important, the coadjutor spoke for him.

Preparations had been made for the consecration of the Highland coadjutor; but emigration and death had so much reduced the numbers of the clergy that Mr. Æneas Chisholm's services as a priest were required during the ensuing winter. Hence his consecration was delayed till the following year.

One of the last vigourous efforts of Bishop Hay was to dictate directions to his trustees regarding his fifty bank shares. His remarkable clearness in calculation showed that his intellect still retained its power, although his memory had so greatly failed.

Meanwhile, the reputation of Bishop Hay's theological works was spreading far and wide. The *Devout and Pious Christian* was now translated into the French language by a French Priest in America, for publication in France; and the translator applied to Bishop Cameron for a biography of the author. This request was forwarded to Bishop Hay, who appeared to be quite indifferent to the proposal. He did, however, give the date of his birth, adding that he was of a "respectable family," that his father had "given him a full education in the medical line," that during his studies he had embraced the Catholic religion, and pursued a full course of theological studies at Rome; that, returning to the mission in 1759, he was consecrated Bishop and coadjutor in 1764, succeeding to the Vicariate in the eastern district of Scotland in 1778. This short notice was all that could be obtained for the zealous translator of his excellent works.

The Bishop was still able to teach the students of philosophy. They were engaged with him in the study of logic and natural philosophy. In these studies the Bishop employed *Pura's Physics* as a text book.

The Bishop and his coadjutor were quite of one mind, contrary to what some people affected to suppose. This pleasing fact is fully established by their confidential correspondence.

The state of the Seminary at this time was very gratifying to the aged Bishop, and gave promise of still greater improvement in the near future. There was favourable harvest weather and an abundant crop. The number of students had increased, and they as well as their masters were in excellent health. In the midst of this prosperity there came a dismal cloud. On the night from 25th to 26th of October, the Bishop, already so infirm, was struck with paralysis. He was unaware of the stroke, until he attempted to rise, when he felt that his right side was affected. He arose, however, and got into his chair, managing to dress himself without assistance. By the time he had done so, he was scarcely able to move or speak. He was immediately put to bed again, and medical assistance sent for. His mind, meanwhile, was not in the least affected. Towards evening, the oppression still continuing, he desired to receive the Viaticum, dreading lest later he should not be able to swallow. All that his physician could do was to recommend warmth and friction. But he himself, remembering that anodyne plaster was used successfully in Spain for paralytic affections, had one applied to his loins. In consequence he passed a good night, sleeping well, and appeared to be better next morning. His speech at the same time was less inarticulate. The plaster having succeeded so well, he applied it to his head and those parts of his limbs which were most affected. The results were excellent. Originally of a strong constitution, he slowly rallied from the attack. By the 30th of October he was able to leave his bed, dress and undress himself, and take his food with tolerable appetite. Next morning he rose at seven, an early hour in the circumstances, but much later than his wonted time. His right side gradually recovered its power, his defective utterance alone remaining. He attributed his restoration, under God, to the Spanish plaster; and he would have no other remedy.

Bishop Cameron continued to receive bulletins from Aquorties until there was no longer cause to apprehend immediate danger. He then wrote, assuring the Bishop that he prayed earnestly for his recovery, and that he also had the prayers and good wishes of his many friends at Edinburgh. The invalid, now so wonderfully convalescent, replied at some length to the kind letter of his coadjutor; giving details of his attack and recovery, which are in every important particular the same as is here set down. Mr. Charles Gordon was employed on the occasion as the Bishop's amanuensis.

As affairs became settled at Rome, Propaganda renewed its liberality; and along with a remittance of 200 crowns, addressed a letter of encouragement to the aged Scotch Bishops (February 9th, 1805), consoling them in their infirmities and congratulating them on having spent the greater part of their lives in the vineyard of the Lord with so much usefulness that they might say to the just Judge with the apostle of the Nations: "*Ronum certamen certavi.*"

CATHOLICS OF SCOTLAND. 751

CAP. LXI.

BISHOP HAY PARTIALLY RESTORED—DEATH OF HIS SISTER—ASKS LEAVE TO RESIGN—THE SAME GRANTED. 1805—CARDINAL ERSKINE, PROTECTOR—OBTAINS FOR MISSION AND SEMINARY A GRANT FROM PROPAGANDA—INJUSTICE OF NEAPOLITAN GOVERNMENT—THE BISHOPS FOR THE FIRST TIME ADDRESSED AS "MY LORDS"—BISHOP HAY TRANSFERS THE WHOLE GOVERNMENT OF THE LOWLAND DISTRICT TO HIS COADJUTOR—BISHOP CAMERON AT LISMORE—CONSECRATED BISHOP ÆNEAS CHISHOLM—CHANGES—REV. ANDREW SCOTT'S CAREER OF 40 YEARS AT GLASGOW COMMENCES—BISHOP HAY GRADUALLY DECLINING—REMEMBERS HIS FRIENDS—IN SEPTEMBER, 1807, SOME IMPROVEMENT—REMOVES TO EDINBURGH—DINES WITH AN OLD FRIEND—SITS FOR HIS PORTRAIT—RETURNS TO AQUORTIES—INDICATIONS OF MENTAL DECAY—STUDENTS FROM SPAIN AT THE SEMINARY—NEW CHURCH AT PAISLEY—JOY OF THE INFIRM BISHOP—IN 1810 HIS ILLNESS RAPIDLY INCREASES—IN APRIL, 1811, RECOVERS FROM A SEVERE ATTACK; BUT MENTAL POWER GONE—BY 14TH OCTOBER HIS LIFE WAS EBBING SLOWLY BUT

SURELY AWAY—NEXT DAY AT SIX O'CLOCK IN THE EVENING THE GREAT BISHOP PASSED AWAY PEACEFULLY, EXPIRING WITHOUT A STRUGGLE—LOSSES OF THE MISSION—DEATH OF CARDINAL ERSKINE—FUNERAL OF BISHOP HAY ATTENDED BY PROTESTANTS AS WELL AS CATHOLICS—HIS PLACE OF BURIAL—WORDS OF REVS. MESSRS. RATTRAY AND JAMES CARRUTHERS.

By March 9th (1805), Bishop Hay had so far recovered his powers as to be able to write a short autograph letter to Bishop Cameron, chiefly conveying the information that his sister, Miss Hay, had lately died, and praying that her soul might be remembered. Owing to the great feebleness of the writer, the writing is weak, blurred, blotted and misspelt.

Employing as his amanuensis Mr. Gordon, one of the masters of the Seminary, the Bishop once more begged permission to resign his office of Vicar-Apostolic, with its onerous duties. He, at the same time, requested a dispensation from the recitation of his office. He applied on this occasion first of all to the Scotch agent at Rome, begging him to make interest for him with Cardinal Erskine. The letter gives, at considerable length, the Bishop's reasons for desiring to resign. The twofold dispensation from the recitation of the Breviary together with the duties of Vicar-Apostolic, was granted on June 16th at an audience of the Holy Father, *Ex audientia S. Smi.*

When Mgr. Erskine became Cardinal Protector a brighter day appeared to have dawned for the Scotch mission and its College at Rome. His Eminence made strong representations in their favour, and not without beneficial results. Propaganda, in its renewed liberality, remitted to the Procurator at Edinburgh a grant of 1,770 crowns; and the College affairs were so prosperous that its debts were in the course of being liquidated in a few months. The Cardinal also had it in view to obtain for the College the long-desired boon of National Superiors. There was a hope, moreover, of regaining the Neapolitan abbacies. It proved vain, however; and to this day they have not been restored. At the founding of the College, Clement VIII. liberally bestowed funds, and moreover, endowed it with an abbey in Calabria, and another near Benevento. Both together produced about £150 sterling yearly. The College remained in undisturbed possession of these benefices until the expulsion of the Jesuits from the Kingdom of Naples. They were, on occasion of that event, seized by the Crown as Jesuits' property. The Neapolitan Government ever since has found pretexts for refusing to restore them. This information was communicated by the agent at Rome to the Bishops, in a letter of 13th of April, 1805. It may be remarked that this is the first letter of those times, in which we find the Bishops addressed "My Lords," the letter ending with "My Lords, Your Lordships' most obedient, etc." It is addressed to the Right Reverend Dr. George Hay ; Right Reverend Dr. John Chisholm ; Right Reverend Dr. Alexander Cameron ; Right Reverend Dr. Æneas Chisholm.

Towards the end of July Bishop Cameron visited Aquorties. Bishop Hay was at that time able to walk with him to Fetternear, two miles distant, and to return on foot after tea, without being much fatigued. Before they separated, the Bishop, in a formal document, transferred the whole government of the Lowland Vicariate to his coadjutor.

Bishop Cameron continued his journey to the Highland Seminary of Lismore, where he consecrated Bishop Æneas Chisholm on the 15th of September. A few days later the annual letters to Rome were prepared and signed, but for the first time without the name of Bishop Hay. And now some noteworthy changes took place. Mr. John Reid withdrew from the mission of Preshome, Mr. James Carruthers taking his place. Mr. Andrew Scott, succeeding Mr. Farquarson, commenced his career of successful labour at Glasgow, which was only closed by his death forty years later. Mr. James Robertson, who had the reputation of being somewhat eccentric, became a professor at the College of Maynooth with the title of doctor.

The Bishop's physical strength appeared to improve. One day in October of this year, he walked to Fetternear in order to see a workman who had been run over by a cart and severely bruised. In less than two hours he returned to the Seminary. His mind was more at ease, the students giving less cause of anxiety than they had done for some time. The masters did all in their power to promote his comfort, providing him with a bell, and adding a double door to his room, which caused all noises from without to be less heard.

In May, 1806, the Bishop's strength was so far renewed that he undertook a journey to Edinburgh. The Bishops of the Highland district were there on his arrival, and his name appears along with theirs in the annual letters which they despatched, as usual, to Rome. Mr. John Gordon, head master of the Seminary, was his travelling companion; and he returned home by Dundee towards the end of May, none the worse for his journey. Three weeks later, however, there came another slight shock of paralysis, which weakened his limbs and temporarily impaired his speech. His vigourous constitution, nevertheless, carried him through. He felt uneasy as to what might happen in the ensuing winter. Meanwhile, he did not forget his friends. In one of his letters he desired to be remembered to his old friend, Dr. Wood, of Edinburgh. He often sent kindly messages to Madame Bonnette, who was now the mistress of a flourishing dancing academy at Edinburgh. In the beginning of August, the enemy made another attack. It was slight, but lasted longer than the former one. He soon recovered through an application of the anodyne plaster. Bishop Cameron showed his concern and his anxiety for the infirm Bishop's welfare, by writing to the Superiors of the Seminary a very feeling letter, in which he urged on all, students as well as professors, the duty of bestowing the greatest care in alleviating the sufferings of the invalid. The same anxiety was manifested by Bishop Cameron on occasion of a visit to the Seminary in the autumn. He gave two of the students written directions regarding their attendance on the infirm Bishop. The latter, hearing of this, asked to see the paper, and appeared to be pleased with it. The young men then requested him to name certain times in the day when they might go to his room and see whether he wanted anything. He did not wish them to come to him too often, as long as he could walk about. They insisted on the instructions of

Bishop Cameron, interpreting them as an order to visit Bishop Hay five or six times a day. He strongly objected to this, saying that Bishop Cameron must have forgotten that he had only to touch the bell for the maid-servant when he wanted anything. The students then dropped the subject, lest they should annoy the Bishop, but continued to visit him every day about noon, again at four o'clock and at seven, the master taking tea with him at five. Finally, the Bishop limited their visits to one, late in the evening, when he desired some good book to be read to him.

In September of this year (1807) Bishop Hay's health had so much improved as to enable him to remove to Edinburgh, in compliance with the advice of his physician, who considered Aquorties too damp a place for an invalid. Mr. Charles Gordon, of Aberdeen, accompanied him on the journey. He resided with Bishop Cameron in High School Yard, now known as Surgeon's Square. One day he was invited to dine with his old friend, Mr. Glendonwyn, and his daughters, at Simson's Hotel in Queen street. The Bishop accepted the invitation and went to dinner attended by a young priest, Mr. Thomson, who was afterwards the missionary priest of Ayr. In the course of the dinner the Bishop asked for a glass of sherry, and the servant, by mistake, gave him a glass of brandy. He had nearly swallowed the contents of the glass before he discovered his mistake. Mr. Thomson laughed aloud. The Bishop rebuked him severely, as he deserved, for his want of manners.

Bishop Hay, throughout his long career, could never be induced to sit for his portrait. He was now at last prevailed on, chiefly through the influence of the daughter of his late highly esteemed friend, Dr. Wood. This portrait, by Watson, is perhaps the best that has been preserved. It has been frequently engraved, and sometimes copied. There is another at the Scotch College of Rome, which was taken on occasion of his visit to the Papal City in 1782, when he was in full health.

The Bishop was much better for spending the winter in Edinburgh. In the first week of April he set out on his return journey to the Seminary, accompanied by the Reverend William Reid, of Stobhall, and later, of Dumfries, where he ended his long career. On reaching Aberdeen the Bishop felt a good deal exhausted, but he was so far restored by his night's rest as to be quite able to continue his journey to Aquorties the following day. On his arrival he gave the students a whole play-day in compliment to his travelling companion. This fact is noticeable as up to that time he had never done so much. It speaks also for the kindly manners of the late Mr. Reid, who had completely gained his good will. Notwithstanding, it occurred to him that the latter was taking care of him, as indeed he was; and he asked him why he was going North. Mr. Reid replied that he was going, in compliance with Bishop Cameron's request, to see how the farm at Aquorties looked. The Bishop was satisfied. But he remarked that if Mr. Reid had been going on his (the Bishop's) account he could have gone quite as well by himself.

There were now indications of that mental infirmity which continued till the final change. He found it difficult to understand why the hour hand of a watch did not go as fast as the minute hand. A few days earlier he mistook the evening for the morning, and instead of going to supper, went to the chapel with his stole on, waiting for Mass and Communion. He was able, notwithstanding, to compose a letter; and he dictated a long one to Mrs. O'Donnell and her husband, expressing his gratitude to them for their kind attention to him during his recent visit to Edinburgh, and assuring them that they had his warmest prayers for their welfare and prosperity.

The number of students at the Seminary was increased this year by the addition of those young men who had escaped from Valladolid under the guidance of Mr. Wallace. They resumed their studies, and their master was appointed to the charge of a class.

Bishop Hay was able to communicate all this to Bishop Cameron. Observing notice in the Edinburgh *Advertiser* of the opening of a new church in Paisley, he made haste to assure Bishop Cameron that every one in the Seminary "was elated with joy on hearing of his success" on the occasion. From this time (1810) the progress of the Bishop's infirmities was painfully rapid. His bodily strength appeared to increase as his once powerful intellect declined. This was shown by a walk he undertook one day to Inverurie, where he remained all night at the inn. Next day it was found necessary to have recourse to a stratagem in order to bring him home. He was placed in a postchaise, ostensibly for going to Edinburgh. Finally it became necessary to employ force in order to prevent him from straying from home. In April, 1811, he was seized with an alarming illness in the night. It appeared so dangerous that Extreme Unction was administered. He rallied, however, before morning and continued to improve, But the torpidity in his countenance and the stupidity of expression were permanently increased. He passed the summer in the state of health now usual to him; but his mental powers were gone. Although now rapidly failing in strength, he was able to walk about a little, until the day before the last. In the afternoon of the 14th of October he was put to bed, and remained totally unconscious till the end. Next day in the afternoon he was anointed by Mr. James Sharp. Life was ebbing away, surely but peacefully, and the great Bishop expired without a struggle at a quarter to six in the evening.

This was a sad year in the annals of the Catholics of Scotland. Bishop Hay ended his extraordinarily bright career in the dismal gloom of mental obscuration; Mr. C. Maxwell was torn by death from the flock that he had served so well; and the mission was deprived forever of the support and invaluable services of the patriotic Cardinal Erskine, who died at Paris.

On the 21st of October took place the funeral of Bishop Hay. It was conducted in the most simple manner. The company walked from the College to the Cemetery. The Protestant community was well represented by Sir Alex. Grant, of Monymusk, Mr. Gordon, of Manar, and Mr. Harvey of Braco, together with the Ministers of Inverurie and of the Chapel of Garioch. There must also be mentioned the presence of Mr. Menzies, of Pitfodels, a chief friend and admirer of the deceased Bishop, and the Rev. John Reid. The students, attired in mourning, walked in procession to the place of interment; and when all was over, the company dined at the Seminary, Mr. Menzies occupying the chair. The place of burial selected was an ancient cemetery picturesquely situated within the park of Fetternear house, on a steep bank round which flows the River Don. Within the enclosure set apart for deceased members of the Leslie family were laid the remains of the departed Bishop. A Chapel has since been erected there; and in the south transept is enclosed the grave of Bishop Hay. The eminent Bishop, who did so much by his indefatigable labours to restore the Catholic religion in Scotland, needs no panegyric. It may not be out of place, however, to quote the words of two venerable priests, which were written in reply to the circular letter announcing the Bishop's death. The Rev. Mr. Rattray says: "The venerable Bishop Hay has gone to receive the reward of his long and faithful labours in the vineyard of Christ. He certainly proved by his learning and his bright example of all virtues, while among us, a most signal blessing to that vineyard; and now, we have every reason to believe, he is where he can and where he will still render it service; for his soul was holy, and most zealous for the divine honour." The Rev. James Carruthers, a meritorious historian, expresses similar sentiments, although in fewer words: "The exit of our most worthy and ever-to-be revered Father, Bishop Hay, although with good reason it has awakened the most lively feelings, was certainly a desirable event. The purification, I trust, was completed, and the veil dropped to afford easy access to the sanctuary. Yet the tribute we pay is exacted by gratitude and justice."

CAP. LXII.

BIRTH OF BISHOP CAMERON—IN HIGH FAVOUR AT ROME—VERY SUCCESSFUL STUDIES—HIS PATRIOTISM—HIS FIRST MISSION, STRATHDOWN—IN 1780 PRINCIPAL AT VALLADOLID—HIGHLY ESTEEMED—IN 1798 CONSECRATED BISHOP AT MADRID—SEVERAL YEARS IN SPAIN OFFICIATING AS BISHOP OF VALLADOLID—COMMISSION FROM COURT OF SPAIN REGARDING THE IRISH COLLEGE OF SALAMANCA—EVERYTHING SETTLED TO THE SATISFACTION OF ALL PARTIES—URGED BY THE COURT OF MADRID TO REMAIN AS A BISHOP IN SPAIN—RETURNS TO SCOTLAND—AT ONCE VICAR-APOSTOLIC OF THE LOWLAND DISTRICT—RESIDES AT EDINBURGH—RESULTS OF HIS LABOURS AND HIS PREACHING—GREAT ABILITY, EXTENSIVE LEARNING AND REFINED MANNERS—PUTS AN END TO A BANK PANIC—BUILDS ST. MARY'S CHURCH—SITE MOST JUDICIOUSLY CHOSEN—FOSTERS THE SEMINARY OF AQUORTIES—REV. ALEX. PATERSON, COADJUTOR—ON OCCASION OF THAT "CAUSE CELEBRE," SCOTT VS. M'GAVIN, BISHOP CAMERON HONOURED BY THE JUDGES OF THE LAND—IN 1825 STRUCK WITH APOPLEXY—IN 1828 ILL AGAIN—IN FEBRUARY OF THE SAME YEAR, A CALM AND PEACEFUL DEATH

ENDED HIS BRIGHT CAREER—BISHOP ÆNEAS CHISHOLM COADJUTOR IN THE HIGHLANDS— SUCCEEDS HIS BROTHER AS VICAR APOSTOLIC— DIED JULY 31ST 1818.

BISHOP CAMERON.

Auchindryne in Bræmar, Aberdeenshire, was the birthplace of this distinguished Bishop. July 28th, 1747, was the date of his birth. His earlier studies were at Scalan ; and philosophy and theology he studied at Rome. He enjoyed great favour in the Papal City not only on account of his great abilities, but also through the influence of Cardinal York. His parentage recommended him to this eminent member of the exiled Royal Family. In 1715 his father held a commission in the army that was raised in the interest of the Cardinal's banished father ; and in 1745, although unable to take the field himself, he sent two substitutes to serve in the army of Prince Charles. Mr. Cameron remained eight years at Rome, pursuing the higher branches of ecclesiastical study. He was eminently successful ; more so than all his class fellows. It is not, therefore, surprising that he won the first prizes, and that the Jesuits, who directed his studies, did all in their power to induce him to join their Society. Notwithstanding the length of time he was at Rome, he was only at the second year of his theology when the scarcity of missionary priests in Scotland required that he should be ordained and undertake duty in his native land. He was, accordingly, raised to the priesthood on the 2nd February, 1772, when he returned to Scotland and was appointed to the mission of Strathavon. There he laboured with great acceptance, gaining the good will and esteem of all, Protestants as well as Catholics, till 1780, when he was nominated Principal of the Scotch College at Valladolid by his predecessor in the Episcopacy, Bishop Hay. There, as in Rome, his superior talents and friendly manners won for him many friends, among whom were the chief characters of the ancient and still important city. Valladolid was then, and it is to-day, the Capital of old Castile. It is also the seat of an ancient and renowned University, of a Court of Chancery, and of a Bishop's See.

There likewise is the residence of the Captain-General of the Province. The opinion and advice of the Scotch rector were often sought and followed in affairs of public importance. On his arrival in Spain he knew not a word of the language of that country; but, under this disadvantage, his ability once more served him well; and he not only learned the Spanish tongue, but also acquired a thoroughly correct pronunciation, so that Spaniards themselves could not from his speech, discover that he was a foreigner. The business of the College required that he should repair to Madrid. He was introduced there to the leading men at Court, and was by them cordially received, especially by Count Compamanes, Governor of the Council of Castile, who ever afterwards treated him with marked attention. In 1797, when the increasing infirmities of Bishop Geddes rendered him unable any longer to exercise his episcopal duties, Bishop Hay proposed Mr. Cameron to fill his place as coadjutor. Briefs appointing him to this office, with the title of Bishop of Maximianopopolis, were received on the 19th September of the year mentioned, and on 28th October, 1798, he was consecrated at Madrid. He remained in Spain for some years after his consecration; and, in compliance with the request of the aged and infirm Bishop of Valladolid, he performed, during the period of his stay, the whole episcopal duty of that diocese. While so acting he was commissioned by the Spanish Court to inquire into and settle very serious differences that had arisen between the rector and students of the Irish College in Salamanca. This commission he executed with consummate prudence and ability. After a patient investigation, he arranged everything to the complete satisfaction of the Court, of the rector, Dr. Curtis, Archbishop of Armagh, and of the students, many of whom afterwards signalized their zeal in the land of their nativity. In 1802, Mr. Cameron, although urged by the Court of Madrid to remain in Spain, returned to Scotland. The whole charge of the Lowland district at once fell to his share, Bishop Hay's infirmities obliging him to resign the office of Vicar-Apostolic. It is not surprising that in the midst of the troubles which surrounded him, he was wont to consider the years that he had passed in Spain as the happiest of his life, and that he often expressed his intention to return to that Catholic country and end his days in the Scotch College. He appeared, however, to have given up this idea some time before his death. He was frequently spoken of at Valladolid, and always in terms of well-deserved praise.

His residence was now at Edinburgh; and the Catholics of that capital and the country generally may well claim to date a new era from the day that he first appeared amongst them as their Bishop. He had indeed entered on a new and very different field from that in which he had hitherto been called upon to act. There was no longer for him the Catholic nation and the friendly court. A cloud of hostile prejudice overhung his native land. The people, still untaught by all the experience they had passed through, cherished their ancient hatred of the Catholic faith. So great an evil, the enlightened

Bishop was persuaded, could only be lessened, if not wholly remedied, by returning, not evil for evil, but, on the contrary, good for evil. To this task the wise pastor applied all his energy. Highly gifted as a preacher, he was indefatigable in spreading instruction. Such efforts were, in a great measure, confined to his parishioners. But through them, and by means of occasional attendance on the part of less bigoted Protestants, his preaching was so far effectual and light was made to shine in dark places. His personal demeanour was even more powerful than his eloquence. It conciliated for him good will in Scotland as it had done in Spain. Respect and admiration increased as his career wore on. His great ability, extensive learning and refined manners, brought him into relation with the higher circles of society and won their esteem, whilst, by rendering himself accessible to all, and by kindly dealing with them, he became a favourite with the more humble classes. The writer has heard the late Rev. Alex. Badenoch relate a circumstance which shows how popular the Bishop had become at Edinburgh. There was a panic at the bank of his friend, Sir William Forbes. Hearing of it, he gathered up whatever money he could find about the house, and hastened to the bank. But *cui bono?* The dense crowd of panic-struck depositors rendered all approach impossible. He succeeded in getting some one to listen to him. This person, on hearing that he was going to bank a few hundred pounds, told his next neighbours; and so it spread among the eager crowd. A way was made and it was seen by all that it was no other than Bishop Cameron who was going to place money in the bank. So prudent a man could not trust his money to a ruined bank. So thought the people; and the panic was at an end.

At the time of Bishop Cameron's accession to office, the numbers and importance of the Catholic people had greatly outgrown their church accommodation. The churches, or chapels as they were called, were almost all of a very humble kind and not sufficiently large to accommodate the congregations that resorted to them. This was a serious hindrance to the growth and even the maintenance of religion. The Bishop laboured assiduously and with all the energy of his powerful mind to remedy this evil; and his success was all that could be expected at the time at which he lived. The Church of St. Mary; Edinburgh, at present in use as the Cathedral of the Archdiocese of St. Andrews and Edinburgh in the restored hierarchy, shows with what judgment, good taste and perseverance he proceeded. The site for this church was admirably chosen near the fashionable dwellings of Picardy Place and York Place, the great highway from Edinburgh to the Port of Leith and the important thoroughfare of Broughton Street. All this, notwithstanding, the Church was capable of being concealed. It was placed fronting Broughton Street, but so far back from it as to admit of a row of dwelling houses between it and the thoroughfare, in case of hostility arising. No such hostility as would have required this precaution ever occurred; and the open ground in front, itself an ornament, allows the handsome façade to be seen. The Bishop, anxious that the church should be in keeping with the improved architecture of the modern capital, had recourse to the services of an architect of known ability and taste, Mr. Gillespie Graham, than whom none was more thought of at the time. This accounts for the really church-like appearance of the edifice, of which it is not too much to say that it was an auspicious beginning of the still more ecclesiastical architecture that came into vogue through the genius and enthusiasm of Mr. Pugin.

Next to providing suitable churches, came the care of finding priests to minister in them. This care was not neglected by Bishop Cameron. In pursuance of it he paid the greatest attention to the Seminary of Aquorties. When the charge of that institution was laid upon him, as coadjutor, by his predecessor, who founded it in 1799, the latter earnestly besought him to watch over its interests. This admonition Bishop Cameron never lost sight of. He was wont to say that "Aquorties was the apple of his eye," and his conduct in regard to it clearly showed that he spoke sincerely. He took care that the Seminary should have pious and learned professors; he furnished the library at great cost with the most useful and approved works, both ancient and modern; he gave special attention to the comfort of the students, and he laid out large sums of money in improving the farm. At last, when he resolved on resigning the charge of the district to a coadjutor, the idea of giving up the superintendence of Aquorties appeared to cost him more than anything else, so great was his solicitude for its welfare.

In 1815, desiring to have a coadjutor, he personally consulted each of the priests as to who should be chosen, and their choice, as well as his own, falling on the Rev. Alexander Paterson, at that time the priest of Paisley, this most worthy clergyman was nominated coadjutor and consecrated Bishop by Bishop Cameron the following year.

On occasion of the case, Scott vs. McGavin, it was shown how little Bishop Cameron trusted to the better feeling of the populace of large towns, and this was as late as the year 1821. Mr. Scott came to

Edinburgh in order to consult the Bishop as to the expediency of prosecuting the man who had grossly calumniated him in a periodical of which the libeller was editor. The Bishop was opposed to prosecution on the ground that there was too much bigotry at Glasgow to find a jury that would convict, however clear the evidence. Mr. Scott represented that if he did not prosecute, he could not remain in Glasgow; and if a verdict could not be obtained, no worse consequence would ensue. Although the Bishop could not approve of bringing an action against the libeller, he did not forbid it to be done; and Mr. Scott proceeded with the case. Bigotry, notwithstanding, there existed, as there always does exist in the minds of the Scotch people, a sense of justice; and the Jury unanimously found a verdict of guilty against the libeller. At the trial Bishop Cameron was examined as a witness. His evidence being concluded, Lord Gillies, the presiding Judge, invited the Bishop, if he wished to remain in Court, to take a seat on the Bench. This was a compliment—a mark of honour —for which the excellent Bishop was not prepared. He was not, however, such a tyro in the ways of mankind as not to accept the learned Judge's politeness. There were extreme people in the Court of the calumniating editor's persuasion, who are said to have been horror-struck. The celebrated Lord

Jeffrey was counsel for Mr. Scott; and distinguished himself by a singularly able speech.

In the closing years of his episcopal career Bishop Cameron was greatly impeded in the exercise of his sacred duties by serious illness. In 1825 he was seized with apoplexy. Few survive such attacks; and in his case it nearly proved fatal. Contrary to all expectation, however, he was soon convalescent; and had so far recovered from the effects of the shock, both as regarded his physical strength and mental power, as to be able to interest himself, as was his wont, in the general affairs of the Vicariate, promoting with all his energy its welfare and prosperity. Three years later the end was seen to approach. On the 29th of January, 1828, he caught cold, as was supposed, and nothing worse was apprehended. But, on the following day, his physician, Dr. Ross, who thoroughly understood his constitution, declared him to be in imminent danger. He was better and worse alternately, for another month. But on the 7th February the great change unmistakably approached, and shortly before midnight of that date, he departed this life in peace, and to all appearance, with little or no painful struggle. He was surrounded till the last by faithful friends, and enjoyed all the consolation that religion could impart. His place of interment was under the Gospel end of the altar of St. Mary's Church, now the pro-Cathedral of the Archdiocese of St. Andrew's and Edinburgh. It is noteworthy, as indicating an improved state of popular sentiment, that the funeral was conducted publicly according to the rites of the Church. It was the first time that such a service, with the appropriate ceremonial, had been performed in Scotland since the " Reformation."

Æneas Chisholm was a native of Strathglass, Inverness-shire. Having completed his studies at Valladolid, he was ordained there in the year 1783. In May, 1785, he became one of the masters of that College; and from thence he was transferred, in 1786, to the College of Douai, where he filled the office of Prefect of Studies till the autumn of 1789, when he came to the mission of Scotland and was stationed in Strathglass. On the first of August, 1803, a postulation was despatched to Rome, praying that he should be appointed coadjutor to his brother, Bishop John Chisholm. In compliance with this request, Briefs nominating him Bishop of Diocesarea and coadjutor Vicar-Apostolic of the Highland district were expedited on the 19th of May, 1804. The scarcity of priests, however, rendered it necessary that he should do duty as a missionary till the 15th September, 1805, when he was consecrated by Bishop Cameron at Lismore. In 1814 he succeeded his brother as

Vicar-Apostolic. His pontificate was not of long duration. There was hardly time to appreciate, as they deserved, his zeal and apostolic labours, when he died at Lismore on the 31st of July, 1818. He was buried with appropriate funeral honours in the Island Cemetery.

CAP. LXIII.

BIRTH OF BISHOP PATERSON—SUB-PRINCIPAL OF HIS COLLEGE BEFORE HIS STUDIES WERE FINISHED—HIS FIRST MISSION, TOMBÆ—IN GREAT HONOUR THERE—DEVOTED TO THE POOR—FOUR YEARS' LABOUR AT PAISLEY—COADJUTOR—CONSECRATED AT PAISLEY—DEPUTED TO RECOVER THE SCOTCH PROPERTIES IN FRANCE—HIS SKILL IN NEGOTIATION FINALLY PREVAILS—RECOVERS ALSO FOR THE IRISH COLLEGE—TRANSFERS THE TWO COLLEGES TO BLAIRS—SUCCESS OF BLAIRS—THREE DISTRICTS IN PLACE OF TWO—BISHOP PATERSON RETAINS THE EASTERN DISTRICT, WITH RESIDENCE AT EDINBURGH—IN 1828 SUCCEEDS BISHOP CAMERON—THE SAME YEAR CONSECRATES REV. ANDREW SCOTT—RECOVERS THE FUNDS IN FRANCE OF THE SCOTCH MISSION—PROMOTES EDUCATION—"CATHOLIC EMANCIPATION"—DEATH OF BISHOP PATERSON—THE EX-KING AND ROYAL FAMILY OF FRANCE, CARDINAL LATIL, BISHOPS SCOTT AND KYLE, TOGETHER WITH OTHER DISTINGUISHED ECCLESIASTICS, ATTEND HIS FUNERAL—APOSTOLIC CHARACTER OF DECEASED BISHOP—BISHOP RONALD M'DONALD—SUCCESS OF HIS EARLY STUDIES—SUCCEEDS BISHOP ÆNEAS CHISHOLM—HIS ACCOMPLISHMENTS—RELIC OF IONA—IONA.

BISHOP PATERSON

Was one of those distinguished ecclesiastics whom the mission owed to the Catholic Enzie. He was born at Pathhead, in that country, in March, 1766. In his youth he spent a year of study at the Seminary of Scalan. At the age of thirteen he entered the College at Douai, and remained there till that house was broken up by the outbreak of the French Revolution in 1793. The great ability of which Mr. Paterson gave proof and the unexceptionable conduct which graced his early years won for him the favour of his seniors; and he was appointed sub-Principal of the College before he reached the end of the time usually allotted to study. On returning to Scotland he was stationed at Tombæ, Banffshire, and remained there till 1812. In the remote district which became the scene of his labours, he was looked upon as nothing less than an oracle, by the Protestant as well as the Catholic community. More than this, he ever showed himself the friend and protector of the poor. In this relation he was powerful, and accomplished much good, having great influence with the Duke of Gordon and other local proprietors. Paisley, where missionary duty was onerous in the extreme, was his next mission. He had been there only four years when he was nominated Bishop of Cybistra and coadjutor, with right of succession to Bishop Cameron. The consecration took place at Paisley. The French Revolutionists, not satisfied with breaking up the Scotch Colleges at Paris and Douai, seized and confiscated all the properties connected with them. It was hoped that under the rule of a more regular government those properties might, in a great measure, be recovered. Here was a field for the diplomatic ability of the learned Bishop. In the year 1821, accordingly, he repaired to Paris and commenced the difficult work of negotiation. He was vigourously opposed by a board consisting of both French and Irish members. But with all their ingenuity and cunning contrivances, they were no match for the skill and diplomatic power of the Bishop. They were completely baffled; and the greatest success possible in the circumstances was achieved on behalf of the mission. All the confiscated property of the Scotch Colleges in France that had not been sold under Revolutionary Governments was recovered. On the same occasion the Bishop bestowed his efforts in regaining for the Irish College its confiscated property, and with the like success.

Bishop Paterson conceived the happy idea of uniting the two Colleges of the Highlands and the Lowlands, in order that there might be one thoroughly efficient College. He lost no time in taking measures for carrying out this laudable design, and he was cordially and ably seconded by the late John Menzies, Esquire, of Pitfodels. This Catholic gentleman liberally presented the fine estate of Blairs, in Kincardineshire, six hundred acres in extent, and beautifully situated on the right bank of the river Dee, six miles from Aberdeen. The mansion house was enlarged and adapted for the purposes of a College. There remained only to transfer to it the establishments of Lismore and Aquorties. This was happily done; and a Seminary for all Scotland was at once in full operation. It was prosperous at its commencement; and it continues to proper. Two Bishops and an Archbishop have already sprung from the ranks of its alumni, together with others who have won distinction in their ecclesiastical career.

It is said to be an evil to multiply princes. But this saying does not apply to the princes of the Church, who are the shepherds of the flock, appointed to guard them and lead them into wholesome pastures. The more they are multiplied, therefore, the better are the sheep of the fold protected and sustained by the salutary food of sound doctrine. Such considerations as well as the actual necessities of the mission called for the presence in Scotland of a third Bishop. With this end in view, the country was divided into three missionary districts. These divisions were termed, respectively, the Eastern,

Western and Northern Vicariates Apostolic. In 1826 the Bishop visited Rome in order to obtain Papal sanction for this arrangement and the appointment of a Bishop. In February, 1828, he succeeded the deceased Bishop Cameron as Vicar-Apostolic of the Lowland district. In September of the same year he consecrated the Rev. Andrew Scott, who became Vicar-Apostolic of the Western district in succession to Bishop McDonald, the Rev. James Kyle appointed Vicar-Apostolic of the Northern district, and reserved for himself the Eastern and not least important division of the country. On occasion of his visit to Rome he was appointed a domestic chaplain to His Holiness the Pope.

The French revolution of 1830 caused the students of the Scotch mission who were pursuing their studies at Paris to return home. Bishop Paterson, regardless of personal danger, proceeded to Paris in September of the same year, in order to save if it were possible the college funds belonging to the Scotch mission from alienation. His success was great, beyond all expectation; so much so that he obtained from the existing Government the same management of the funds in question that he had exercised under the reign of Charles X. In consequence of this arrangement the students were enabled to return to Paris and recommence their studies.

During the last three years of his life the Bishop resided chiefly at Edinburgh. Notwithstanding the various occupations that necessarily claimed his time, he was able to keep the Church in good repair and even add to its decorations. The cause of education had its due share of attention. None understood better how advantageous sound education was to the Catholics of his charge and the rising Church of his country. At the period of his untimely death he was engaged in devising measures for the improvement of the Catholic schools and establishing them in a state of greater efficiency and respectability.

The final deliverance of the Catholics of the United Kingdom of Great Britain and Ireland from almost all the remaining legal disabilities took place during the pontificate of Bishop Paterson. The "Catholic Emancipation Bill," as it was called, passed through both Houses of Parliament and received the Royal Assent, after having surmounted all the difficulties that were thrown in its way, by the still existing bigotry of the country. It was at last conceded to the fears, rather than granted by the liberality and good will of Parliament. The words of the Duke of Wellington leave no doubt as to this unpleasant historical fact. In moving the second reading of the bill in the House of Lords, the Duke of Wellington said: "My Lords, I am one of those who have probably passed a longer period of my life engaged in war than most men, and principally, I may say, in civil war; and I must say this, that if I could avoid by any sacrifice whatever, even one month of civil war in the country to which I am attached, I would sacrifice my life in order to do it. I say there is nothing that destroys property and prosperity and demoralizes character to the degree that civil war does; by it the hand of man is raised against his neighbour, against his brother and against his father; the servant betrays his master, and the whole scene ends in confusion and devastation. Yet, my lords, this is the resource to which we must have looked, these are the means to which we must have applied in order to have put an end to this state of things if we had not made the option of bringing forward the measures for which I hold myself responsible." The eminent statesman, Sir Robert Peel, in his memoirs, corroborates the testimony of the immortal Wellington: "I can with truth affirm, as I do solemnly affirm in the presence of Almighty God, to whom all hearts be open, all desires known, and from whom no secrets are 'hid,' that in advising and promoting the measures of 1829, I was swayed by no fear except the fear of public calamity, and that I acted throughout on a deep conviction that those measures were not only conducive to the general welfare but that they had become imperatively necessary in order to avert from interests which had a special claim upon my support, the interests of the Church and of institutions connected with the Church—an imminent and increasing danger."

The great change, with its accompanying circumstances, must now be recorded. On Friday, 28th October, 1831, Bishop Paterson left Edinburgh for Dundee, in order to conduct the services in the latter city on occasion of a contribution being raised towards the funds of the Infirmary of that place. On the following Sunday the Bishop celebrated and preached after Mass. The Church was crowded, many respectable Protestants being present. The Bishop's dignified appearance in his gorgeous episcopal robes, together with his earnest words, produced a most favourable impression. His text was from that passage of the prophet psalmist; "*Blessed is he who considereth the poor; the Lord will deliver him in time of trouble.*" He made a powerful appeal to the feeling of his audience in favour of the excellent Institution in behalf of which he was preaching. Speaking of the liberality which distinguished the management of this Institution, he said: "Thanks to the liberal enactments of our Legislature the day has now gone by when it was enquired of our suffering fellow-brethren, whether they were Protestant or

Catholic." In another part of his sermon, as if anticipating what was so soon to happen, he said: "Let not your hearts be deluded by the love of that wealth which perisheth, let not your eyes be dazzled by the glittering of gold or silver. All these shall soon pass away. You and I shall soon have to appear before the tribunal of the Sovereign Judge to give an account of the use which we have made of the mammon of this world; and nothing shall remain except what we shall have employed in relieving the miseries of the distressed." Towards the close of his discourse, which was about three-quarters of an hour in length, his voice began to falter. Nevertheless, he was able to conclude with a glowing eulogium of the Infirmary, and insisted on the necessity of contributing towards the relief and comfort of those who, though now laid on a bed of sickness, had perhaps seen better days. He withdrew from the pulpit a little after one o'clock. On entering the vestry, he complained of a violent pain in his head, and a few moments later he exclaimed: "O God, I am dying! O God, have mercy on my soul." In five minutes more, he was speechless. A physician was speedily called, who bled him profusely; but the bleeding gave him no relief. The Sacraments of the dying were then administered; and at twenty minutes past four o'clock he expired, thus departing to his reward, whilst humanely and charitably labouring to promote the relief of the poor and afflicted.

In compliance with the wish of the deceased Bishop's friends, his remains were conveyed to Edinburgh, with the purpose of being laid at rest in his own church. An apartment of the Episcopal residence was appropriately prepared; and there, according to the rites of the Church, the body lay for some time, arrayed in pontifical robes with mitre, cross, ring and crosier. Among the numbers who came to pay a last tribute of respect to the departed were the ex-King, Charles X., and the Royal Family of France. The funeral service was performed in St. Mary's Church; and so great was the desire to be present that it was found necessary to issue tickets of admission. His Eminence Cardinal Latil and the Right Rev. Bishops Scott and Kyle participated in the solemn obsequies. The Rev. William Reid, assisted by the Rev. John Murdoch, afterwards Bishop in the West, and the Rev. James McKay, who died lately at a very advanced age, celebrated the Mass of Requiem. The Rev. Alex. Badenoch, with the fine feeling for which he was remarkable, delivered an appropriate funeral discourse; and when all the ceremonies prescribed by the Ritual were concluded, the body was reverently consigned to its final resting place.

It is but justice to Bishop Paterson to say that he assiduously employed his abilities, which were of a high, if not perhaps of the very highest order, in promoting the good of the Church and the welfare of his fellow-Catholics. He was of the strictest principle, and never swerved from what he believed to be true and just. He generally formed his resolutions with exquisite judgment and carried them out, not unfrequently in the face of formidable opposition, with unflinching firmness. His negotiations in regard to the Scotch property in France, which proved so successful, showed that he was possessed in no small degree of diplomatic skill. At home the simplicity of his life, his kindly manners and truly apostolic character, gave him an influence which nothing could resist. He was an enemy to controversial disputation, which seldom results in conviction, but, on the contrary, widens the breaches already unhappily existing between Christians. Such discussions are scarcely ever conducted with that coolness and regard to charity, which alone could render them useful and instructive. Hence, the venerable Bishop believed that they militated against that mutual forbearance and good-will among all classes and denominations which he constantly preached.

RANALD M'DONALD, (1820-1832).

This Prelate, although born at Edinburgh, was of Highland parentage. In very early life he was sent to the Scotch College of Douai. He there passed through the usual course of study in a most creditable manner, becoming an excellent classical scholar. As soon as his studies were completed he was ordained priest and returned to his native country. From this time (1782), till he was raised to Episcopal dignity in 1820, he ceased not to discharge with exemplary zeal and more than ordinary ability the onerous duties of a missionary apostolic. His first station was in Glengairn, Aberdeenshire, where he laboured for a few years and was thence transferred to Glengarry. His next mission was in the Island of Uist, where there was a numerous and scattered congregation. On the demise of Bishop Æneas Chisholm he was nominated Bishop of Aeryndela and Vicar-Apostolic of the Highland district. The Briefs appointing him were issued in autumn, 1819, and he was consecrated Bishop by Bishop Paterson at Edinburgh towards the end of February, 1820. During his Episcopate he led a very secluded life; but never lost that grace of manner which distinguishes the Christian gentleman. Although remote from what is called Society, he possessed more true refinement than many of those who spend their lives in the highest circles. His attainments as a scholar were of the highest order; and, even in his old age, he could write and speak Latin with the utmost facility, purity and elegance. It was due to his literary acquirements that he was frequently called upon to act as secretary at the meetings of the clergy. Although it adds nothing to the merit of the accomplished Bishop, it is, nevertheless, illustrative of his time that he possessed a relic of Iona—Iona, that was so long the abode of the Apostolic Saint Columba, and whence he so often went forth to preach the Gospel to the barbarian Picts; Iona, that for centuries spread the light of religion, like a glory, over the surrounding lands; Iona, where for many generations were sepulchred the Kings of Scotland, and where lesser potentates, the Kings of the Isles, were often laid at rest with all the honours usually done to royalty; Iona, that, impervious to time and war, survived the depredations of the heathen Dane; Iona, the very thought of which and its holy associations so moved the critical mind of Doctor Johnson that he exclaimed: "That man is little to be envied whose devotion would not grow warmer amid the ruins of Iona!" Iona, the odour of whose centuries of excellence still hangs around its ruined walls; Iona, a place of pilgrimage, to which repair devout Catholics in order to offer up their prayers and renew their fervour at the fallen temple and the broken shrine; Iona, the scattered stones of which, as if endowed with the eloquence of Columba, proclaim aloud the long discarded truth to an unbelieving nation.

CAP. LXIV.

GLENGARRY PRESENTS TO BISHOP M'DONALD THE GOLDEN CHALICE OF IONA—INTERESTING ACCOUNT AND DESCRIPTION OF THIS ANCIENT RELIC—BISHOP M'DONALD BECOMES VICAR-APOSTOLIC OF THE WESTERN DISTRICT—THE COLLEGE OF LISMORE TRANSFERRED TO BLAIRS—BISHOP M'DONALD HIGHLY ESTEEMED—BISHOP SCOTT COADJUTOR—STUDIED AT SCALAN, DOUAI AND ABERDEEN—HIS FIRST MISSION, DEECASTLE—AFTERWARDS AT HUNTLY—IN 1805 PASTOR OF THE IMPORTANT CONGREGATION OF GLASGOW—THE HONOURABLE AND RIGHT REVEREND BISHOP M'DONALD—RAPID INCREASE OF GLASGOW'S CONGREGATION—HOSTILE PREJUDICES—ARDUOUS AND TRYING LABOURS—MR. SCOTT RESOLVES TO BUILD A CAPACIOUS CHURCH—A COMMERCIAL CRISIS IMPEDES THE WORK—THE PERSEVERANCE OF MR. SCOTT FINALLY SUCCESSFUL—THE NEW CHURCH FREQUENTED BY GREAT AND IMPOSING NUMBERS.

It was certainly a high privilege to possess a relic of Iona. It was the good fortune of Bishop McDonald to enjoy this privilege. Through the favour of his friend, Alexander Ranaldson McDonell of Glengarry, he became the possessor of a chalice of gold which had served ten centuries, it is believed, in the Monastery of Iona. It must now be shown how the precious relic came into the hands of Glengarry. His ancestor, in the time of King Charles II., was requested by his neighbour, McLean of Dewart, to assist him against some chief with whom he was at war. Glengarry, who, at the time, enjoyed the title of Lord McDonell and Aros, complied with the request, and proceeded, with five hundred of his warriors, to the assistance of his friend. On his arrival in McLean's country, he was honoured with a banquet, at which were used certain pieces of church plate, and among the rest, the chalice of Iona. Glengarry was shocked at this profanation of sacred things, and determined to return home, saying that no success could attend the arms of people who were so profane. McLean, on learning this, sent all the plate, as a present and propitiatory offering to Glengarry, beseeching him to remain and bestow his aid. The offended chief was so far propitiated as to allow his men to stay with McLean, but refused to remain himself, and immediately returned home. The chalice was safely held in the Glengarry family till the time of Alexander, already mentioned, who presented it to Bishop McDonald. A description of this remarkable chalice will be found in Principal Sir Daniel Wilson's work, "Pre-Historic Annals of Scotland." A letter quoted in that work from the late Rev. William Gordon (the last head of the Glenbucket family) to the writer of these sketches, says that it was of solid gold, and evidently of great antiquity, as could be seen upon it the marks of the hammer which had beaten it into shape. The invaluable relic, associated with which were so many interesting memories, continued in the possession of Bishop Ranald McDonald until the end of his days, when it passed to his successor, Bishop Scott.

In 1826, Bishop Paterson had succeeded in obtaining the division of Scotland ecclesiastically into three Vicariates, designated as the Eastern, Western and Northern Districts. This measure, considering the circumstances and state of the missions, had become not only expedient, but necessary. On occasion of the change, Bishop McDonald became Vicar-Apostolic of the Western district, which comprised a considerable portion of the Highlands, which still remained under his jurisdiction. Thus, his title was changed, and, to a certain extent, the scene of his episcopal labours. About the same time he was relieved of the care of his Seminary at Lismore, that institution becoming united, chiefly through the agency of Bishop Paterson, with the College for the

Lowlands, now transferred from Aquorties to Blairs, on the river Dee, near Aberdeen, a property bestowed for the purpose by the late John Menzies, of Pitfodels.

Notwithstanding this partial relief, the labours of the Episcopate were so arduous that Bishop McDonald found it necessary to have a coadjutor. His choice fell on the Rev. Andrew Scott, whose merits were at once recognized by the clergy and the authorities at Rome. He was accordingly consecrated Bishop and entered on his duties as coadjutor Vicar-Apostolic of the Western district. Bishop McDonald, meanwhile, by his amiability of manner, and his kindness of heart, had won the esteem and affection of all, whether Catholics or Protestants, who came into relation with him. Such were his benevolence and attention to all around him that his society was much sought, and gave the greatest pleasure. He rejoiced in contributing to render others happy; and he found a source of happiness himself in diffusing cheerfulness and promoting innocent enjoyment. It is easily conceived, as is recorded of him, that he was greatly beloved as well as respected by persons of all persuasions. Some of the most eminent ministers of the established Kirk of Scotland were of the number of his personal and devoted friends. Hence, he did more by his way of life and conversation, as his record bears witness, to do away with religious prejudices and mitigate theological antipathies than any other man of his time. Towards the close of his life, unfortunately, he became almost totally blind. In consequence of this affliction, his coadjutor came to be invested with independent authority in governing the district. At last came the closing scene. The venerable Bishop departed this life on the 20th September, 1832, at Fortwilliam, Invernessshire. The Right Reverend Bishop Scott, assisted by several priests of the neighbourhood, paid the last funeral honours and laid his remains at rest within the Catholic Church of Fortwilliam.

ANDREW SCOTT (1828-1846).

"There is the making of a priest in that little fellow." Such were the words, which proved prophetic, concerning Andrew Scott, when only five years of age, spoken in his father's house by an elderly missionary priest. The intelligent look of the "little fellow" elicited this remark; and it was to him as an oracle which he treasured up in his mind and never forgot. From that moment he resolved to be nothing less and nothing else than a priest, whatever impediments might be thrown in his way. He was a native of the Catholic Enzie, and born at Chapelford, on the 13th day of February, 1772. His application to study in his earlier years was attended with remarkable success. In February,

1785, he became an alumnus of the Seminary at Scalan, and was soon after sent to continue his ecclesiastical studies in the Scotch College at Douai. He resided there several years, and was distinguished no less by proficiency in his studies than by piety and edifying conduct. The French Revolution came, and he was obliged, along with his fellow students, to return to Scotland. He then once more became an inmate of the only Seminary in Scotland, the unpretending House of Scalan. His course of study for the priesthood was, however, completed at Aberdeen, under the guidance of the Rev. John Farquarson, formerly Principal of Douai College. He was ordained priest in that city by the venerable Bishop Hay, on the 25th day of March, 1795.

The missionary labours of Andrew Scott, which were destined to be so important, had a very humble commencement. As soon as he was ordained he was appointed to the retired mission of Dee Castle, in Aberdeenshire. The poor congregation then had, at the time, no suitable place for the celebration o public worship. There were on the banks of the River Dee, the ruined walls of an ancient castle. These walls Mr. Scott contrived to fashion into a church. Having thus gained experience in the art of architecture, he afterwards built a modest, but convenient chapel and dwelling house under the same roof. In 1800 he was removed to the charge of the Huntly mission; and, as if five years were his destined time in each of the minor missions, he was appointed in 1805 to the mission of Glasgow, which, by this time had grown to large proportions, and which, through the truly Herculean labours of its new apostle, was destined so soon to surpass in numbers and importance all the missions of the country.

Previously to the appointment of Mr. Scott, the few Catholics of Glasgow were ministered to by the Reverend Alexander McDonell, who afterwards became the founder of a church in the new world, and was long known as the Hon. and Right Rev. Bishop of Kingston, in Canada. When this eminent priest proceeded on his new destination the Glasgow congregation came under the pastoral care of the Rev. John Farquarson. This zealous priest erected a church in the district called "the Calton." Although, at this time, Catholics were becoming numerous in Glasgow, they were under the necessity of living as retired as possible, such was still the danger, notwithstanding the better feeling towards them of the more intelligent citizens, lest the very fact of their numbers might become a cause of popular excitation. There were no traces of their religion in the villages and counties around the great commercial city, if unless, indeed, we except the wreck of the cathedrals, monasteries, religious and educational houses that once adorned the land.

Meanwhile, Catholic Ireland contributed largely, as it still contributes, to promote the growth and importance of the Glasgow congregation. Mechanics of that country—skilled and unskilled workmen—sought the Scotch commercial city in order to find that employment which their native land denied them. The cotton trade had been successfully introduced into Glasgow, and hence those people found the occupation they so much needed. The new trade gave them their bread, and to the city wealth and aggrandizement. The Irish comers were at first exposed to much obloquy, not only on account of their country against which there existed an incredible amount of illiberal prejudice, but, more particularly still, on religious grounds, there being nothing so odious as "Popery" to the Presbyterian mind of the time. Such prejudices, however, proved only an ineffectual check; and the industrious Irish, encouraged by the more enlightened manufacturing citizens, continued, to flock into Glasgow, bearing with them the light of their reviled faith, which was destined, ere long, to shine amid the darkness and command universal respect.

To form these ever increasing elements into a well-disciplined, orderly and united congregation, was the gigantic task that lay before the zealous missionary; and he applied to it with all the strength and energy of a giant. The very inadequate church accommodation of that time was a serious impediment. A sort of garret chapel in a miserable, dingy lane connected with a street called the Gallowgate, was all the place of meeting which the Catholics possessed. Their numbers had increased; but they were far from being the imposing congregation which now consists of so great a proportion of the population of the immense commercial city. The list of Easter communicants amounted only to four hundred and fifty. Not many years had passed when it swelled into a roll of three thousand. This wonderful success was achieved partly by the earnestness and vigour with which Mr. Scott ceased not to preach the word of God; but more, perhaps, by his assiduity in hearing confessions and in visiting the sick. Such duties were far from being easily fulfilled. To sit the whole evening till a late hour, under a damp unwholesome roof, listening to the recital of the sins and cares and sorrows of his people, was sufficiently trying, but it was more so still, through the darkness of night, and often in the most inclement weather, to toil along the streets and lanes to the most wretched hovels of the poor, bend over the fever-stricken, in danger every moment of inhaling the poisoned breath of pestilence, and confronting death itself while mitigating its terrors. It is impossible to imagine a more trying, and at the same time, a more consoling labour. And well it was that it should bear with it its consolation and its fruit ; for, in the case of Mr. Scott, the only reward the world offered consisted of the sneers and taunts of bigotry, the scoffing of the ungodly and the hooting of the ignorant rabble. There was no security often against personal violence, except through the escort of some faithful friend. Every day new difficulties arose, but only to be surmounted by undaunted courage and success. Not the least of these was one occasioned by the necessities of the mission, and which it behoved the zealous priest to meet. The Calton Chapel, as it was called, had become too small for the greatly augmented congregation. Thousands of poor Catholics were excluded from its narrow precincts, and, as each succeeding Sunday came round, instead of participating along with their brethren in the joyful celebration of the Sacred Mysteries, could think only in sadness and disappointment of the land of their fathers and its numerous altars where so many joyfully partook of the Bread of Life. The narrow and humble chapel must be replaced by a capacious church. But how was this to be done? Only Mr. Scott could conceive the possibility of such a work. Relying on the generosity of his numerous but comparatively poor congregation, his own energy and the aid of Heaven, he undertook the building of St. Andrew's Church in a conspicuous part of the great city—Great Clyde Street. There were many, meanwhile, who, taking credit to themselves for superior wisdom, condemned the undertaking as rash and inconsiderate, and which could only tend to humiliation and the injury of religion. The goodly work, nevertheless, was boldly undertaken, and proceeded with rapidity and success while scarcely any other aid was bestowed save the pennies of the poor, so liberally offered in ever-increasing abundance. This liberality was the more noteworthy as a great commercial crisis had overtaken Glasgow. Public credit was shaken, business came to a stand, wages were reduced, and the price of food increased. The Catholics were dismayed. They looked with sorrowful eyes on the unfinished walls, and dreaded their becoming a ruin instead of growing into a stately church. One alone was not discouraged. Mr. Scott still persevered, hoping against hope. In a short time, notwithstanding all but insuperable difficulties, the sacred edifice was completed, and stood forth a noble monument of apostolic zeal and the devoted generosity of a Catholic people, while. if it did not excel, it was not unworthy of the splendid minister which survives entire the wear of time and the violence of fanatic rage. There was no mistaking the proof which this labour of love afforded, that the Catholics of Glasgow could no longer be treated as outcasts whom it was safe to jeer and insult. They now assembled in imposing numbers. The thousands that poured every Sunday from the grand portal of St. Andrew's Church, were indeed a type of that Universal Church which the beloved disciple beheld in prophetic vision.

CAP. LXV.

EDUCATION AT GLASGOW—A FAR SEEING MEASURE—EMINENTLY SUCCESSFUL—A CELEBRATED TRIAL SCOTT VS. M'GAVIN—JUST VERDICT—SEVERE PAROCHIAL LABOUR—MR. SCOTT EQUAL TO THE OCCASION—TEMPORAL BUSINESS—RELIEF OF DISTRESS—MR. SCOTT, COMFORTER OF THE AFFLICTED AND FRIEND OF THE CLERGY—A TROUBLESOME ASSOCIATION—THE SAME DECLARED ILLEGAL ON THE AUTHORITY OF DANIEL O'CONNELL—SCHISMATIC ALSO AND HERETICAL—MR. SCOTT HIGHLY ESTEEMED—THE DEFENDER OF HIS PEOPLE—HIS SUCCESS AS LEGAL COUNSEL.

While the Catholics of Glasgow were rejoicing over the successful completion of the house of God there arose another want which caused no slight anxiety to the zealous pastor. There were no means for educating the numerous children of the flock. Hundreds of them were clamouring for the bread of instruction; and there was none to break it to them. Hence, in a manner, coerced, Mr. Scott was obliged to choose between the certainty of vice and some degree of danger as regarded purity of faith. The measure he adopted was, indeed, a bold one; and did not remain unquestioned. By many it was even declared to be inadmissible. The experience of many years, however, has pronounced in its favour—shown that it bore not with it the dreaded evil, while it resulted in incalculable good, and proved to be the resolve of a far-seeing and no ordinary mind. An offer had been made of Protestant co-operation, on condition that the Protestant version of the Scriptures should be introduced into the schools that were to be established. As the teachers were to be members of the congregation who could point out to their pupils and warn them as regarded the passages of the Protestant Bible complained of by Catholics, and which tended to sustain a few of the Protestant views, the faithful pastor found it less difficult to overcome his reluctance to allow the objectionable version to be read in the schools; and, rather than see so many children, the hope of his rising flock, abandoned to ignorance and vice, he gave his consent. The result was that many of those that were without, came forward with donations of money and books, making at the same time, kind and liberal speeches on the grand subject of dispensing unto all the blessings of education. There appears to have been no difficulty in having Catholic teachers appointed; and, for the first time since the days of Knox, there existed Catholic schools at Glasgow. This was indeed a great and most beneficial achievement. Far from corrupting the faith of the Catholic youth, it gave to the future a well-instructed congregation, every member of which was prepared " to give a reason for the faith that was in him." Extensive school premises were obtained in Portugal Street and permanently secured to religion, being converted into a church under the invocation of St. John. Meanwhile, they were admirably adapted to receive the numerous children that flocked to them. Such was the " Gorbals School," as it was called. It soon became insufficient to accommodate the great number that the love of instruction brought from all parts of the city. Hence several other Catholic Schools came to be established in the districts of Anderstown, Bridgetown Calton, Cowcaddens, and North Quarter.

It was now the lot of the good priest of Glasgow to encounter a new and most serious trouble. One Mr. Gavin, a native of Ayrshire and a rigid Presbyterian, who had tried all sorts of trades and passed through a strange variety of fortune, settled, at length, for a time, in Glasgow as the editor of a publication called *The Protestant*. This publication was very unsparing in its attacks on Catholics. It was encouraged in its evil course by a newspaper of the place, the Glasgow *Chronicle*. This journal, in July, 1818, threw out some sarcastic and libellous remarks which were afterwards repeated by *The Protestant*, regarding an Oratorio for a charitable purpose, which took place in St. Andrew's Church soon after it was finished. The Rev. Mr. Scott was accused of "extorting money to build his chapel by a sort of poll tax from the starving Irish, and that by the fear of future punishment. Let the means by which that house was reared be inscribed upon its front, and it will remain for ages to come, a monument of Popish hard-heartedness and cruelty." Again: "The house that is building west of the Chapel, and which is, it is said, intended for the manse, will be large enough to accommodate a dozen of priests, while they remain unmarried, as they must always do; from which I infer that Mr. Scott either has, or intends to have, abundant assistance in milking and managing his flock. It is doubtful how far he exhibits the character of a faithful pastor, while he seems to care only for himself. He asked no answer or explanation from his flock; it was for himself as an individual." Mr. McGavin also published that "Father Scott refused to baptize the children of several labourers (whose names, unfortunately for himself, he specified) until they contributed towards the building of the new Chapel and paid up all their arrears; and that the masters of certain public works were applied to, to retain the weekly earnings of

Catholic employees to aid the erection of the said Roman Catholic Chapel."

Such calumnies could only be swept away by a successful prosecution. But, considering the state of the public mind at Glasgow, what hope was there of success in prosecuting? Bishop Cameron, when consulted, declared that he could see none; and hence endeavoured to dissuade Mr. Scott from submitting the matter to a jury selected from the most prejudiced people in the country. He did not, however, forbid to prosecute; and Mr. Scott, remarking that he must either do so or abandon his mission, resolved to bring an action against his defamers. The damages were laid at £3,000. The chief detractor, meanwhile, encouraged by the great bulk of the less educated classes, who were guided only by blind prejudice, shouted defiance, considering himself secure. It was a most trying and anxious time for Mr. Scott. His best friends dared not venture to give an opinion in his favour. He stood alone, but was undaunted and determined. The ablest barrister of the time, the celebrated Jeffrey, was retained as his counsel; and applied to the work before him with no less earnestness than ability. His speech at the trial was a consummate masterpiece of forensic oratory. Bishop Cameron, who, after giving his evidence, had been invited by the presiding Judge to take a seat on the Bench, could not refrain from complimenting the eloquent counsel, and remarked that his able discourse must ensure success. Jeffrey, surveying the Jury, where there was not much *respectability* to be seen, expressed much doubt. There was, however, unconquerable honesty and a sense of justice which no want of education and no amount of false teaching could ever eradicate from the minds of the Scotch people, even in the humblest walks of life. The twelve jurymen, after hearing the charge of the Right Honourable William Adam, Lord Chief Commissioner, retired for rather more than an hour. A little before five o'clock in the morning, they returned into Court, and unanimously found for the pursuer, against the defender, William McGavin, damages £100; against the defender, William Sym, Clerk of the Glasgow Fever Hospital, £20; and against the defenders, Andrew and James Duncan, printers in Glasgow, one shilling. Mr. McGavin's damages, together with his law expenses, were computed at £1,400. The twelve ordinary Glasgow jurymen, it has been well remarked, "in spite of the prejudices of their education, in spite of their religious antipathies, in spite of the fierce controversies of the day, in spite of all the means used to excite their anti-Catholic feelings, when it came to the point threw their prejudices to the wind, stood to immortal justice, and vindicated the cause even of a Catholic priest."

Mr. Scott could now, with an undisturbed mind, devote himself to the fulfilment of his parochial duties. These duties were necessarily very onerous, the congregation being so numerous and scattered over the increasing city of Glasgow. In visiting the sick and hearing confessions the zealous pastor was most assiduous, as well as in preaching frequently in a crowded church. At all times, but particularly when epidemics raged, visiting the sick was very trying and even dangerous. Mr. Scott was not to be dismayed. Typhus fever, small pox, even the dread cholera morbus had no terrors for him. He was always found when required, whether in the day time or the dead of night, by the bed side of the dying, speaking words of consolation and administering the grace-giving sacraments. If we may judge by the wise instructions which he imparted to the clergy, he did not neglect such precautions as prudence dictated, and on the utility of which science has pronounced. He advised the priests who assisted him to carry with them camphor or other disinfectants, to remain only as long as necessary near persons stricken with infectious or contagious disease, to refrain, as much as possible, from inhaling new air, when in a sick room, to avoid swallowing saliva and to wash their hands immediately after visiting an infected person. The propriety of this last recommendation was well shown by a case which occurred at the Edinburgh Infirmary. A medical student there had neglected, after attending to a typhus fever patient, to wash his hands, as was the custom of the house. He was immediately seized with the terrible fever and died, exclaiming: "O, had I but washed my hands! had I but washed my hands!"

It was scarcely less safe, after great exertion in the pulpit, to sit for hours, often till a late hour in the evening, hearing confessions in the newly built church. This was fearlessly done; nevertheless. The iron constitution of Mr. Scott was proof against every trial.

It fell to the lot of Mr. Scott to transact a great deal of temporal business in connection with his important mission. His punctuality in making all necessary payments and his judiciousness in the outlay of money won for him a golden name among all with whom he came to have business relations. Nor did he neglect the poor. His hand was ever open for the relief of distress. Even his good natured, unstudied salute in the streets was cheering to his more humble friends. But this was nothing to the kindness and charity which gave comfort to the disconsolate and shed a halo over the gloom of the scaffold. His tact and wisdom in ruling the extensive mission committed to his charge could not be surpassed. There was a certain manliness and at the same time *bonhomie* in his manner which few could resist. It was the result of his essential uprightness, and caused his friendship to be so precious and his counsels so valuable to his brother clergymen.

In 1825 a set of illiterate people called the Catholic Association, gave great annoyance to Mr. Scott. These people published a pamphlet in their defence, and inveighed against what they called "the unwarrantable, unprovoked and very surprising attack" of the Rev. A. Scott and the Rev. J. Murdoch, pastors of the Glasgow Catholic congregation. They remarked also on being excluded from all knowledge of the state of the funds or the management of the temporalities, and pointed out a plan for obtaining their *right* in this respect. This precious Association originated through the mistaken zeal of some Irish members of the Church, and became the cause of the endless vexations which ever since that time have beset and annoyed the national bishops and priests in the West of Scotland. Several news sheets were enlisted in their service. Mr. Scott thundered against them in the pulpit, and in a style not the less vigourous for being peculiarly his own. He pronounced the Association illegal on the authority of Daniel O'Connell; and declared, moreover, that all meetings held independently of and in defiance of their pastors were schismatic and heretical. In a memorial or requisition for the redress of grievances, which they sent to Bishop Cameron, they complained that Mr. Scott had attacked them from the pulpit, calling them by the most offensive names and representing those who signed the requisition, as "illiterate rag-a-muffins," comparing the roughness of their handwriting to their "tattered coats," and recommending them, if they had any money to spare to use it in purchasing old clothes to cover their naked members. He declared, moreover, that he knew little of them, but by the scandel they had given to religion.

Although there were a few rebels who gave trouble, Mr. Scott was greatly revered by the congregation generally. He was a strict disciplinarian, and it not unfrequently behoved him to rebuke offenders. But even they who quailed beneath the lash of his just indignation, lost not confidence in his goodness; and had recourse to him when occasion required, with undiminished trust and affection. He was ever ready to defend his people when any difficulty occurred from the real or supposed state of the law. An instance or two may prove not uninteresting; Some of his flock had been summoned to qualify as Burgesses, and were told that if they did not, their shops would be shut. But, on presenting themselves, they were called on to take an oath which implied an abjuration of their Faith. Upon this Mr. Scott took the matter in hand, and visited, more than once, the Dean of Guild in his Court. This official gave proof of extraordinary ignorance of the law, as did, also, his legal adviser. Such lawyers of the city as were supposed to possess some liberality, were asked to act on behalf of Mr. Scott's friends; but none of them could be induced to take up the case. The burden, therefore, fell on Mr. Scott, who proved the actual state of the law, and at the same time threatened legal proceedings against the ignorant authorities. He thus caused his congregation to be fairly treated, and complete justice to be done.

CAP. LXVI.

"NEVER HAD A CATHOLIC TO HANG"—THE ROTHESAY CICERONE—"A SACRAMENTAL SATURDAY"—THE STORY OF WITHERINGTON—MR. SCOTT, BISHOP—BOTH PORTIONS OF THE WESTERN DISTRICT UNDER HIS CARE—GREAT LABOURS—CHURCHES PROVIDED IN HIGHLANDS AND LOWLANDS—BISHOP SCOTT'S LEGAL KNOWLEDGE—SETTLES A LONG PENDING DISPUTE—CHURCHES AND MISSIONS MULTIPLYING—CONSEQUENT INCREASE OF EPISCOPAL DUTY—CONVENT OF THE GOOD SHEPHERD—SACRILEGEOUS THEFT—REV. JOHN MURDOCH, COADJUTOR—BISHOP SCOTT RETIRES TO GREENOCK—HIS DEATH ON 4TH DECEMBER, 1846—RIGHT REVEREND JAMES KYLE, FIRST BISHOP OF THE NORTHERN DISTRICT—HIS LEARNING—RETIRED LIFE—GOLDEN JUBILEE—DIED AT PRESHOME IN 1869, AGED 80.

An execution was about to take place. Mr. Scott attended the condemned man and prepared him to meet his fate. When the day of execution was near at hand, it occurred to a Presbyterian minister and to the magistrates that it would be contrary to use and wont, as well as to propriety, if a Catholic priest were seen publicly on the scaffold. The priest was nowise disposed to leave the soul of his parishioner to "heretical care" in his last moments, and objected to the services of the minister on the occasion, firmly declaring that "he would never consent to any such iniquity." A magistrate was then, after serious consultation, deputed to remonstrate with the refractory priest. The Bailie's (alderman's) odd reasoning was in the following terms: "Mr. Scott," he said, " I have never in all my life, known of a Catholic priest being on the scaffold at an execution." "For this reason," replied the undaunted Mr. Scott, "that you never had a Catholic to hang yet." " But if you persist in this determination, it will cause much talk, give great offence, and not one shilling more will be subscribed by any Protestant to your new chapel." " Nae mater ; I canna help that, nor the like'o' that ; I maun dae my duty ; and you'll alloo me to tell ye that I sall dae it tae ; na, nae threats 'll frichten me, Bailie." The good priest kept his word ; and it may be stated, as showing what narrowness still prevailed at Glasgow, no Protestant ever after contributed a sixpence.

In familiar lectures to his congregation, Mr. Scott exposed the calumnies which Protestants usually indulged in. In connection with this practice, the following anecdote is related : A man named Gillis, the cicerone of St. Mary's ruined church at Rothesay, was wont to play on the credulity of tourists. In pointing out the holy water stoup this man informed inquiring travellers that the Papist Bishop of Glasgow came, every year, and washed his face in it. One day that Dr. Scott was at Rothesay, he accompanied some friends to see the interesting ruins. As the cicerone talked, he listened patiently, and, giving a hint to his friends, he said to Gillis: "Aye, and dae ye ken the Papist Bishop O'Glasgae?"—"Hoot aye, fine that, when he comes, he winna lat me see what he is gaun to dae, but tells me to stan oot by there till he's dune." "Aweell man," quoth the Bishop, "yer this day in a snorl; for I'm the Papist Bishop you've sae aften seen come to wash his face, an tauld the folk aboot; here's a saxpence for yer trouble."

It happened that some members of the congregation had their shops open or did some work about them on a "Sacramental Saturday." On this account they were summoned to the police office. Mr. Scott undertook their defence, and disposed of the case in a manner that was at once summary and satisfactory. When he appeared at the bar of the police court he reminded the magistrate that the "sacramental fast" was imposed by nothing more than Ecclesiastical Law and that any violations of it could be punished only by Ecclesiastical pains and penalties. He, therefore, called on him to inflict only such punishment. To this kind of infliction Catholics could have no objection.

No notice of the Rev. Andrew Scott would be complete without the following story. It is found in all the memoirs of the illustrious Prelate and related on his own authority: A man named Witherington, a native of the north of Ireland and an Orange Protestant, having lost what property he owned at home, came over to Scotland, and by ill luck fell into the company of thieves and depraved persons, some of whom were nominal Catholics. As for himself, he had never once been in a Catholic chapel. He dreamt one night that he was chased by devils along the salt market of Glasgow, and ran for shelter into a house where on entering he found a man who he afterwards understood was a priest, engaged in saying Mass. Hearing the noise of Witherington's sudden entering the priest turned round and bade him be comforted, for as soon as he had finished he would accompany him home. This he did, both of them walking together along certain streets of Glasgow towards Witherington's lodgings. He awoke before reaching them. He thought little of the dream at the time, but, nevertheless, related it to his companions. Sometime after he was persuaded by two or three of them to accompany them to the Catholic chapel in Glasgow, which was the only one at that day, and served by Mr. Scott, the only priest. Witherington and his companions seated themselves awaiting the entrance of the priest and the beginning of the service. When the sacristy door opened and Mr. Scott came out, Witherington started, uttered an exclamation, and whispered to his companions that he saw the man in the strange dress whom he had seen in his dream. He listened attentively to all that was said, and recited his own prayers with some devotion. He was so far impressed as to take a resolution to amend. In a week or two, however, his good purpose was forgotten and he returned to his evil courses. Some time later, he was arrested for an aggravated robbery, committed between Ayr and Kilmarnock, and was conveyed to Edinburgh to be tried. He was convicted, and, according to the custom of the time, condemned to death. It was determined that he should remain in the jail of Edinburgh till the day before the execution, when he was to be taken back to Glasgow and thence, on the fatal morning, to the spot where the robbery had been committed. His route through Glasgow to the jail was the same as he had taken when flying from the devils in his dream. His way from the jail was the same as that by which the priest had conducted him towards his lodgings. Witherington's accomplice in the robbery, also under sentence, was a Catholic. The Rev. Alex. Badenoch, one of the priests of Edinburgh, attended him. Witherington begged to be instructed. As the day of the execution approached it was arranged that Mr. Scott should accompany the convicts out of Glasgow, and that Bishop Paterson, who was then in charge of the Paisley mission, should take his place and attend them on the scaffold, as the place of execution lay in his mission. The day before their last the prisoners were removed to Glasgow. Bishop Paterson and Mr. Scott visited them in the jail. Witherington's cell was a dark one; but the moment Mr. Scott entered it the convict accosted him by name. When asked if he knew the priest, he replied although he had never before spoken to him he should know his face among a thousand. On learning the arrangements for next morning Witherington burst into tears. When pressed to tell the cause, the poor fellow with difficulty related his dream and entreated Mr. Scott to go with him all the way. To this the good priest consented, and encouraged and comforted the humble penitent at intervals on the awful journey, finally inspiring him with the hope to obtain mercy from the Eternal Judge.

Whilst Mr. Scott laboured with astonishing success in promoting the cause of religion, he was, at the same time, its brighest ornament. A true and faithful shepherd, he was always at his post and ever watchful to guard his flock when danger arose, and vigourously defend its members when ungenerously attacked, as was often the case in those days of ignorance and narrow-mindedness. Such merit as his could not be overlooked. It was resolved, accordingly, that he should be elevated to Episcopal dignity. The advancing years of Bishop Ranald McDonald rendered it necessary that in his extensive district he should have the aid of a coadjutor. His brother Bishop of the Eastern District joined with him in petitioning to this effect, and the Holy See, acceding to their wishes, in 1827 appointed Mr. Scott Bishop of Eretria and coadjutor, with right of succession, to the Right Reverend Bishop McDonald in the newly constituted Western District. The consecration took place in St. Andrew's Church, Glasgow, Bishop Paterson officiating, assisted by Bishops McDonald and Penswick.

The new Bishop continued to reside in Glasgow, advancing, with his usual energy, the work of religion in the Lowland portion of the Western District, which may truly be said to have been the result of his own indefatigable labours. Towards the end of 1832 the management of the whole district devolved on him, in consequence of the death of Bishop McDonald. He was not less mindful of the Highland than of the

Lowland portion of his charge. Churches were needed in many parts of the Highlands; and the ever-active Bishop lost no time in providing them. This important work cost him many journeys and much labour. But meanwhile North Morar, Glengarry, Morven, South Uist and Benbecula, Badenoch, Fort Augustus, Arlsaig, and last, but not least, Glencoe, were supplied with suitable churches. In alluding to the last-named place, Bishop Gillis, in his funeral sermon, recalling a too memorable fact of history, thus spoke of the celebrated valley: "To thee, also, he gave an altar of expiation, red vale of mourning, long widowed Glencoe!" It must not be supposed, however, that the Highlands, so dear to the Catholic heart, absorbed all the care and energy of the Apostolic Bishop. New missions at the same time were springing up throughout the Lowlands. Religion, freed from her cruel bonds, appeared to be resuming possession of her ancient strongholds. New churches arose in Airdrie, Newton Stewart, Houston, Barrhead and Duntocher, whilst many others were improved and enlarged. So much successful work was, in great measure, due to the Bishop's wonderful ability in the transaction of business. Nothing was overlooked or omitted by him that required his care and judicious consideration. Disputes and difficulties were avoided by the pains which he took in writing contracts. They were submitted, moreover, to the scrutiny of his "man of business" (legal adviser), although his own knowledge of law was, not unfrequently, found to surpass that of his learned attorney.

Bishop Scott's knowledge was great; his soundness of judgment, if possible, greater still. His sense of justice was no less complete; and these qualities being universally recognized throughout England and Ireland as well as Scotland, it was considered safe to appeal to him in cases of the greatest difficulty. The long standing dispute between the English secular clergy and the powerful Benedictine Order was referred to him for final settlement. He took the whole case into consideration, and after mature deliberation gave his decision, which was accepted without a murmur by both seculars and regulars.

The addition of the Highlands and Western Isles to his Episcopal care greatly increased his apostolic labours; and he never shrank from them, meeting them all with his wonted energy. Neither the most fatiguing journeys by land, where no conveyance could be used, nor the waves and storms of the wild Atlantic, were any hindrance to his unconquerable activity. He beheld only the desolation of many Highland missions, and used every effort to render them prosperous and flourishing. His solicitude for the Highlands did not, however, diminish his care of the Lowland country. As has been seen, missions and churches multiplied through his zeal; and the progress which he inaugurated is still a remarkable feature of the West of Scotland. There was wanting, as yet, an Ecclesiastical Seminary. The Bishop, anxious that there should be a sufficient number of clergy trained at home, purchased the estate of Dalbeth, near Glasgow, with a view to establish there a College for his Vicariate. There was on the estate a finely-situated mansion house, which, the Western District having its share in the College of Blairs, together with the other two districts, is now devoted to a more urgent want, that of the Convent of the Good Shepherd.

The Bishop in the midst of his success met sometimes with serious mortifications. Such was the sacrilegious theft of the chalice of Iona, which he had inherited from his predecessor, Bishop McDonald. One night that the safe for keeping the altar plate of St. Mary's Church was left unlocked, thieves broke into the vestry, and carried off the precious relic. It was afterwards found, but, cut to pieces, ready for the melting-pot. (See Cap. on Bishop McDonald, and Sir Daniel Wilson's Pre-historic Annals of Scotland.)

From 1833 Bishop Scott enjoyed the aid of a coadjutor, who was no other than the Right Reverend John Murdoch, whose career, afterwards, as Vicar-Apostolic, was so brilliant. By 1836, the venerable Bishop's health was so much impaired that he felt himself to be unequal to the ever-increasing business of Glasgow and the surrounding country. In order to obtain some relief he retired to the less laborious field which the town of Greenock presented. He continued, nevertheless, to devote himself to the care of his numerous flock. But the duties which he still performed were too arduous for his decreasing strength, and, finally, broke down his vigourous constitution. The illness which proved to be his last, was of long duration. It is believed to have originated in the damp vestries of his church at Glasgow, when, as yet, but newly erected. It could not be otherwise than unwholesome to remain for hours in those vestries, hearing confessions, after great exertions in the pulpit every Sunday. But the danger of illness could not deter him from giving the comfort and consolation of his ministry to his numerous penitents. Years and labours at length did their fatal work. The good Bishop sank gradually to his rest, giving no sign of intellectual decay save, occasionally, a slight and momentary wandering of the mind. He was perfectly resigned to the will of God, and made over, without a murmur, the staff of his authority to his successor, begging, at the same time, his forgiveness for leaving him so much to do. This was, indeed, although he thought it not, pronouncing his own eulogium. He died at his residence, Shaw street, Greenock, on the 4th December, 1846, aged seventy-four years and ten months. His funeral took place at St. Mary's Church, Glasgow, Bishop Gillis preaching on the occasion an appropriate and eloquent sermon.

All Bishop Scott's sermons, admonitions, warnings, and exhortations to his people were delivered in the old Scotch dialect. He must have done so for greater edification, for none could write or speak better English, as is shown by some sermons of his composition which are preserved at Greenock.

The first Bishop of the Northern District, the Right Reverend James Kyle, was born at Edinburgh on the 22nd of September, 1788. He studied at the Seminary of Aquorties from 1799 till 1808, when he was appointed to a professorship in that Institution. He was promoted to the priesthood on the 21st of March, 1812. During the long period that elapsed between that time and January, 1826, he continued to act as a Professor at Aquorties. He was then stationed at St. Andrew's, Glasgow. He was not long engaged in that laborious mission when his Superior next caused him to be called to the Episcopal office. On the 13th February, 1827, were received in Scotland the Briefs by which he was nominated Bishop of Germanicia and Vicar-Apostolic of the newly-constituted Northern District. His consecration took place at Aberdeen in September of the following year. He lived to enjoy his golden jubilee; and, what is not a little extraordinary, it was celebrated in Glenlivat, and not at Preshome, his favourite residence, and which had been so long the chief seat of the missions of Scotland. All the time that could be spared from the faithful discharge of his Episcopal duties he devoted to the collection of manuscripts and printed papers connected with the history of the country and the Church. He enjoyed the reputation of being one of the best antiquaries of his time. It is matter for surprise that, with all his ability and knowledge, he never gave any writing to the public. The writer has heard him say that his only contribution to the annals of the land must be facts; and that he left it to those who should come after him to present them in the attractive style of finely-written history.

The long and useful career of this learned Prelate came to an end at Preshome in 1869, when he had reached the advanced age of eighty.

CAP. LXVII.

BIRTH OF THE RT. REV. ANDREW CARRUTHERS—CHOOSES THE ECCLESIASTICAL STATE—STUDIES AT DOUAI—HIS RETURN TO SCOTLAND—PREFECT AT SCALAN—COMPLETES HIS STUDIES AT ABERDEEN—ORDAINED PRIEST ON 25TH MARCH, 1795—IN CHARGE OF BALLOCH MISSION—CHAPLAIN AT TRAQUAIR, AT MUNSHES AND DALBEATTIE—MUCH REVERED—EXTENDS THE MISSION—HIS GARDEN—AN AMATEUR CHEMIST—CLASSICAL STUDIES—RETIRED LIFE—ATTENDS A MEETING—VICAR-APOSTOLIC OF THE EASTERN DISTRICT—NINE MISSIONS; AND TEN PRIESTS—BUILDS ST. PATRICK'S CHURCH, EDINBURGH—MORE CHURCHES—ANNAN—CHURCHES AND CLERGY MORE THAN TREBLED—ST. ANDREW'S SOCIETY.

Bishop Paterson was succeeded in the Eastern Vicariate by the Right Reverend Andrew Carruthers. This Prelate was born at Glenmillan near New Abbey in the Stewartry of Kirkcudbright on the 7th of February, 1770. He was of a highly respectable antient family that had persevered in the Catholic Faith amidst all the trials and persecutions of the last and preceding century. His early education was acquired in the quiet and retired village near which he first saw the light---a village famed for the romantic scenery around it, and for its time honoured abbey which still remains in its ruins a noble monument of the glories of a bygone age. As if catching inspiration from the mouldering pile, young Carruthers was wont in his boyhood to wander up and down the shattered aisles and to explore every hidden nook of the sacred place. This remarkable taste, together with the thoughtful and serious turn of mind which he so early displayed, won for him among his playmates the name of the "young priest." The grace of Heaven crowning his natural disposition, his future destiny may be said to have been then determined on; and so, his devout parents consenting, he made his choice and dedicated himself to the service of God in the Ecclesiastical state.

With a view to carrying out his laudable purpose, and after having acquired some knowledge of the Latin and Greek classics, he entered in the sixteenth year of his age the Scotch College of Douai. In the course of the six years that he remained there he gave proof in the public schools of the University of that place astonishing progress in every branch of literature and science. He was already well advanced in his theological studies when the terrible Revolution, which broke out in France in 1792, obliged him to abandon them for a time, and to make his escape along with others of his fellow-students to his native land. He arrived there, at length, in safety, after having encountered great difficulties and incurred much danger. On his return to Scotland he was appointed Prefect of Studies at Scalan. He was noted there for the perfect order and discipline which he maintained, and after a short term of office he went to complete his theological studies at Aberdeen, under the guidance of the Rev. John Farquarson, formerly Rector of Douai College. In due time he was advanced to the priesthood by Bishop Hay. His ordination took place on the festival of the Annunciation, 25th March, 1795.

Mr. Carruthers, immediately after his ordination, was placed in charge of the laborious misson of Balloch. Within the range of this mission were Drummond Castle, so long the residence of the Dukes of Perth, and the town of Crief, together with the Highlands of Perthshire. The Catholics, although few in number, were widely scattered throughout these mountainous regions; and, notwithstanding the difficulties they had to contend with in fulfilling the duties of their religion, had faithfully adhered to it during the most trying times. The young priest was most zealous in the discharge of his duties towards this devoted remnant of his fellow-Catholics. He afforded them the consolation of numerous visits and frequent administration of the sacraments of the Church, travelling on foot from house to house, through the beautiful glens and mountain passes of the country.

In 1797 he removed to Traquair in Peebles-shire. There his duties were less onerous, but not less faithfully fulfilled. He acted as chaplain to the noble family of the Stewarts, Earls of Traquair, and as missionary priest among the Catholics of the neighbouring country.

It appeared to be the destiny of Mr. Carruthers to move southwards. In three years more towards the end of 1800, he was appointed to the mission of Munshes, in his native county. Munshes was the seat of an ancient family, still Catholic, at the time of this appointment. There were to be exercised not only the duties of family chaplain, but at the same time the more laborious charge of the numerous Catholics of the neighbourhood who assembled for the public offices of religion in the chapel of Munshes House. There the priest resided until some years later, the property falling to Protestant heirs, and the domestic chapel, besides, being too small for the congregation, he removed to the neighbouring village of Dalbeattie, where, in 1814, he expended a portion of the funds left to the mission by Miss Agnes Maxwell, the last Catholic who held the estate of Munshes, in building a church and house on a piece of ground which he had acquired for the purpose.

As may be well supposed Mr. Carruthers quitted with regret the hospitable mansion of Munshes, where he and his predecessors had been so kindly maintained for generations, and the cause of religion encouraged and upheld. During the two and thirty years that he presided over the mission in his new home, he was a most assiduous but unostentatious labourer in the spiritual field confided to his care. He was diligent, particularly in instructing the young and causing the members of his congregation generally to fulfil the duties of religion. He had a certain sternness of manner, which, instead of being a hindrance, rather facilitated the maintenance of discipline. His horror of all wickedness was so well known that his very frown was a terror to evil doers. Meanwhile he failed not to cultivate the amenities of social life; and hence became a favourite among the leading characters of the country and the people generally. Such were the reverence and propriety that he caused to be observed in the house of God, that perfect silence prevailed during the celebration of Mass; so much so that not even a cough came to disturb the solemnity of the holy service. His mission extending during twenty-five years, to the whole Stewartry of Kirkcudbright with the exception of a small portion near Dumfries, and as far into the county of Wigton as the Irish channel, it may be conceived what a load of duty was imposed upon him. In so wide a district, there were several congregations requiring his attendance. There were stations which he formed at Kirkcudbright, the county town, at Gatehouse and Parton in the one county, and Newton Stewart in the other. All these stations he visited regularly during his incumbency, with the exception of Newton Stewart, to which the Rev. Dr. Sinnot was appointed in 1825. An idea of his arduous labours may be conceived when it is stated that one of the stations was forty miles distant from his home, another twenty miles, and none of them less than twelve miles, and that now, four priests are employed in attending to the duties which it fell on him so long to fulfil alone.

Mr. Carruthers, notwithstanding his multifarious spiritual occupations, found leisure to improve the rugged piece of land around the church and house which he had built. In this he was eminently successful. In the rocky parts he planted shrubs and plants of various kinds; and, the more level places, where there was any soil, he adapted for flowers and vegetables. He was an excellent botanist and took great delight in cultivating a variety of the most beautiful flowers. Every portion of his garden was very tastefully laid out, in so much that he acquired in the neighbourhood the two-fold reputation of being an admirable gardener and landscape gardener. His work became an object of curiosity and attraction throughout the country; and whenever there was a pleasure ground, a plantation, an avenue, a shrubbery or garden to be planned he was invariably consulted.

He had in early life acquired a knowledge of experimental philosophy. Chemistry, in particular was his favourite study; and he failed not at intervals to cultivate this science during his missionary career and indeed, throughout his whole lifetime. He was generally very successful in the chemical experiments, which he made, as often as he had time for them. He took care to acquire the most recent publications on the subject of his favourite study. He thus became aware of every discovery at the earliest moment. When resident at Blairs College, he took pleasure in imparting to the students a taste and liking for the philosophical pursuits in which he himself took so much delight.

It might be supposed that so practical a man cared little for literature. Letters, nevertheless, were an additional source of pleasure to him. The ancient Greek and Latin classics, as well as the modern literary authors, were quite familiar to him;

and he possessed that refinement of taste which adds so much to the pleasure of such studies. He wrote Latin with ease and elegance. Nor did he ever forget the French language, which he had learned so well during his earlier years in France. Although he never revisited that country, he could still speak French with ease and fluency, his diction and pronunciation being singularly correct. He was possessed of remarkable conversational power, and varied information, and an inexhaustible store of anecdote caused his society to be much sought. When called upon unexpectedly to speak on public occasions, his remarks were always happy and to the purpose. During his long sojourn in Galloway he enjoyed the esteem of Protestants as well as Catholics. The former, notwithstanding his different creed and uncompromising, though unobtrusive defence of it, sought and courted his acquaintance and society.

Mr. Carruthers lived quite retired during the long period of his missionary career, and was in consequence little known beyond those portions of the country where duty required his presence. He had scarcely any acquaintance with his brother priests, especially in the northern part of the country, which, at the time, constituted the Lowland District. The remoteness of his residence in great part accounts for this. It is no matter of surprise, therefore, that he took no part in the questions which concerned the general state of the missions; nor that he did not attend any of the meetings of the clergy till the year 1827. In that year he was present at the annual meeting of the friendly society which was held at Huntly. On that occasion, by the judicious and timely remarks which he made on the various subjects that came under discussion, he produced a particularly favourable impression on the meeting and won the esteem of many to whom he had hitherto been quite unknown. He resumed, on returning home, his usual routine of duties, little imagining that he was to be torn from his beloved retirement and placed in a more prominent position, exchanging the care of a comparatively small portion for the charge of the whole Eastern district.

There was now a delay of two years in filling the place vacated by the death of the much regretted Bishop Paterson, who, in 1827, had obtained from the Holy See a new partition of the Ecclesiastical jurisdiction of Scotland and the establishment of a third Vicariate. The seat of this Vicariate remained vacant until 1832, when the Vicars-Apostolic of the Western and Northern Districts, with the unanimous concurrence of the clergy, addressed a supplication to Pope Gregory XVI., requesting the appointment of Mr. Carruthers to the vacant

Vicariate. Briefs, accordingly, were issued on the 13th of November, 1832, nominating him Bishop of Ceramis *in partibus infidelium*, and Vicar-Apostolic of the Eastern District. The consecration took place in St. Mary's, Edinburgh, on the 13th of January, 1833, the Right Reverend Dr. Penswick, at the time Vicar-Apostolic of the Northern District of England, officiating as consecrating Bishop, assisted by the Right Reverend Drs. Scott and Kyle, Vicars-Apostolic of the Western and Northern Districts of Scotland.

Mr. Carruthers was far from coveting the dignity to which he was now raised. On the contrary he accepted it reluctantly and only from obedience. His first care was to make himself acquainted with the circumstances of the flock to the charge of which he was appointed. There were but few missions in his district and few clergy. The number of the former was nine; and that of the latter ten. There were only eight chapels or churches, and no reasonable hope of any immediate accession to the ranks of the clergy. Funds, besides, were wanting for the erection of additional churches. The Catholics, meanwhile, were increasing in numbers, although not much in opulence. The prospect was anything but bright. Nevertheless, the new Bishop, relying on the grace of Heaven, did not shrink from the arduous duties that lay before him, and zealously applied to the task of improving the various missions, as far as circumstances and the means at his disposal would permit. His labours began in the capital. There, with the aid of a gift of money from the late Mr. Menzies of Pitfodels, a munificent benefactor of the missions generally, he erected the handsome church of St. Patrick, chiefly for the accommodation of the Catholics resident in the "old town." The clergy, meanwhile, were not idle. Sustained by the encouragement which the Bishop gave them, and not unfrequently by his active co-operation, they succeeded in raising churches in several important centres. Among these were St. Andrew's (1836) and St. Mary's (1851) Dundee. Stirling and Falkirk were favoured with churches and houses for the clergy, chiefly through the exertions of the late Rev. Dr. Paul McLachlan, distinguished as a controversial writer, with all the aid the Bishop could afford. The churches of Lennoxtown, of Campsie and Arbroath were built under the immediate superintendence of the Bishop himself. He also caused an ex-Episcopal church to be purchased at Portobello, and houses that were converted into temporary churches, at Forfar and Kirkcudbright while a site for a church was acquired at Leith. Annan, an outpost of the mission of Dumfries, was not forgotten. The writer of these sketches being at the time assistant priest at the latter place, it was his duty to visit its dependencies. At Annan there was no better place of worship than a room at an inn. There was in the place an unoccupied church which the writer thought might be acquired. The Rev. William Reid, the senior priest, concurred in his view; the Bishop gave his countenance, and several Catholics their money. Mr. Marmaduke, Constable Maxwell, of Terreagles, subscribing £50, his brothers, William, Peter, Henry, Joseph, also giving handsome sums. Funds were thus provided, the church, a substantial stone and lime building, purchased, and adapted to the purposes of Catholic worship. A projection from the south side was converted into a house, according to a plan made by Mr. M. Maxwell, of Terreagles. All this, although there had never previously been any attempt to set up a Catholic establishment at Annan, appeared only to give pleasure to the inhabitants, who, it may be mentioned here, were well known to entertain liberal and tolerant sentiments. Of this they gave additional proof on the day of the opening when they attended in great numbers, listening attentively to the sermons that were delivered by the coadjutor Bishop (Right Reverend Dr. Gillis), and the assistant priest. The day of opening was a memorable one at Annan. There never before had been so many Protestants at a Catholic celebration. The Catholics were also fairly represented. The Laird of Terreagles and other friends, together with the eminent Bishop Gillis, in these days coadjutor of the Eastern Vicariate, being present.

Annan is here mentioned at some length as it is a place of no slight celebrity. It was the parish, according to Presbyterian forms, of the renowned Edward Irving, who being deprived for entertaining non-Presbyterian views, formed a congregation for himself in London, and astonished that capital and the Empire by his extraordinary eloquence. The non-Presbyterian Church which he established still exists, and is known as "the Catholic Apostolic Church."

Annan, after some time, became a separate mission. The house planned by Mr. Maxwell is still used as the priest's residence. The Reverend Lord Archibald Douglas, of the Queensbury family, is the present incumbent.

Thus was the state of the district slowly but very materially improved. The number of the clergy and churches or temporary buildings where the faithful could assemble, was more than trebled. In all this important work the Bishop was substantially aided by charitable grants from "St. Andrew's

Society." The object of which was to afford support to the poorer missions. Its funds were maintained by collections in the churches and donations by all who took an interest in its work.

CAP. LXVIII.

COADJUTOR APPOINTED — RELIGIOUS SISTERS INTRODUCED — CHAPEL AT MURTHLY CASTLE — COUNTY OF FIFE — RIOT AT DUNFERMLINE — POWER OF THE LAW — LIBERALITY OF PRINCIPAL INHABITANTS — CONDUCT OF THE BISHOP — SCIENCE PATRONIZED — PRESENT TO GREGORY XVI. — SERMONS AT LAWRENCEKIRK TO A PRESBYTERIAN CONGREGATION — REMARKABLE RESULT — PROGRESS AT EDINBURGH — CHARITABLE AND EDUCATIONAL INSTITUTIONS, INDUSTRIAL SCHOOLS, ETC. — THE BISHOP A CLASSICAL SCHOLAR — ECCLESIASTICAL WRITERS — THE QUIGRICH — ITS RESTORATION TO SCOTLAND.

The Bishop now being advanced in years and less able to bear alone the burden of so great a charge resolved to apply for a coadjutor. The choice fell on the Rev. James Gillis, whose appointment was obtained from the Holy See in 1837. He was consecrated as Bishop of Limyra on the 22nd July, 1838. This appointment added new vigour to the administration of Bishop Carruthers. Through the exertions of the coadjutor a colony of religious Sisters was brought from the diocese of Luçon in France, and established at Edinburgh. This was the first time since the great religious revolution that any attempt was made to bring a religious community into Scotland. It was eminently successful. The French sisters, together with an addition to their number from Scotland, at once formed two houses; one, where the teaching of children of the more wealthy classes was undertaken, and another where the Sisters taught the poor and also visited and nursed the sick. They are still known by the name which they originally adopted, that of "*Ursulines de Jesu.*"

The pontificate of Bishop Carruthers was further illustrated by the erection of a beautiful private chapel in the park of Murthly Castle, the seat of the late Sir William Drummond Stewart, the well known American traveller. The Catholics of the neighbourhood were freely admitted to this chapel, and, thus, was founded a mission which still continues. On the accession to the estate of Murthly, of Sir William's brother, who was a Protestant, the chapel could not be any longer used for Catholic purposes. Its furniture and decorations were removed, partly to Crief, and partly to Bankfoot in the neighbourhood where the mission still exists, wholly unconnected with the new baronet's mansion.

The extensive county of Fife may be said to have been annexed, in a missionary sense, to the missions already existing, during the pontificate of Bishop Carruthers. Soon after this county was opened as a field for missionary labour, six stations were established at the most suitable places—at Dunfermline, the chief city of the Western Division of the county; Cupar, the chief town of the Eastern Division; Kirkcaldy; Lochgelly; Newburgh and Culross. The two last named have been discontinued as they were only opened for the benefit of railway people, contractors, clerks and labourers. Churches have since been erected at Dunfermline, Lochgelly, Kirkcaldy, and St. Andrews. At the commencement of these missions much favour was shown to the priest on duty by the Protestant inhabitants generally. The more intelligent even extended their favour to the Irish parishioners. A riot having occurred, the object of which was to expel all persons of Irish origin from Dunfermline, the clerk of the Lord-Lieutenancy, there not being a sufficient police force in the place, caused the military to be called out. A troop of dragoons accordingly, fifty in number, arrived before night, at Inverkeithing, where the Irish people came to a stand, under the protection of the Provost of the old town. They were escorted by the military back to Dunfermline; and as it was late when they arrived, they were lodged for the night in the city hall, the principal citizens bringing for their comfort mattresses, blankets, rations, ale, etc., whilst the magistrates assured them that for the time to come they would have complete protection, the outraged law, although, for once, taken by surprise being more powerful than any force of rioters. The Bishop on the occasion gave proof of his solicitude. Having heard of the riot, he was seen next day in the midst of the agitated city, seated on a bench in front of the principal hotel. A rash scribe boasted, in writing, that the incumbent's congregation was dispersed and that he would henceforth have to preach to empty benches. This was easily denied. There was no difference in the attendance at Mass on the Sunday following the riot. This fact the priest in charge communicated to the editor of a friendly paper who gladly published the statement. Not only on this occasion but at other times as well the incumbent of that day, who was the first resident priest in the county, could congratulate himself on the kind attention shown by the Provost and Magistrates of Dunfermline, the Procurator fiscal and the Sheriff substitute (County Judge) in particular.

The Bishop, now having a coadjutor who shared with him the burden of the Episcopate, was more at leisure to apply to scientific studies. Chemistry was still his delight. He possessed all the more recent works on the subject, and he frequently experimented with marvellous success. Not only this. He extended his patronage to such as interested themselves in chemical pursuits. Mr. Kemp, a working chemist of Edinburgh, had fallen upon a great improvement of the electro-galvanic battery. The Bishop visited him, made a trial of the improved battery, and ordered one for the College of Blairs and another for the Scotch College at Rome. Mr. Kemp then asked the Bishop whether he might presume, when sending to the Scotch College, to send a battery as a present to the Holy Father, Gregory XVI. The Bishop considered that such a present would be very acceptable. A battery, accordingly, was sent to the Pope. Gregory XVI. received it most graciously, and caused it to be operated by a learned professor in his presence. He was delighted; and in order to show his appreciation, sent two beautiful gold medals to Mr. Kemp. These medals were brought to Scotland by the Rev. John Gray, afterwards Bishop of Glasgow, and faithfully delivered to Mr. Kemp.

Meanwhile, missionary duties were not neglected by the Bishop or by the clergy. In this connection it may be told that something entirely new in the history of missionary action occurred about this time. Hitherto it had been found expedient to conduct Catholic services and preach Catholic sermons as privately as possible considering the preju dices that still lurked in the public mind. To attack those prejudices boldly and openly was looked on as an impossibility. The Protestants themselves were the first to overthrow this idea. When the writer of these sketches was temporarily in charge of the Forfarshire missions, the people of Lawrencekirk (a village celebrated as the birthplace of the philosopher and poet, Beattie,) and neighbourhood requested him to come to their village and deliver to them a "Catholic sermon." This request was renewed, from time to time, for several months. At last the priest believing that the good people were perfectly in earnest, consented to preach to them. A very numerous congregation from the village and surrounding country came to hear the sermon. The misrepresentations of Protestant writers and preachers were dwelt upon and the true doctrine of the Church set forth. At the conclusion of the discourse, came thanks and congratulations, together with a pressing invitation to return and give them another sermon. This invitation was frequently repeated during the following two months. The priest taking with him quite a number of the books and pamphlets published by the Catholic Institute of London, repaired to Lawrencekirk and delivered a sermon to a more numerous congregation. He distributed to the audience the Catholic works which he had brought with him; and not without a successful result. A minister of the Scotch Episcopal Church, who was a good deal in advance of his brethren, commenced lecturing against Catholics. The people remonstrated. His defence was that the priest was only deceiving them in order to gain their favour. This assertion they triumphantly repelled, stating that they had standard Catholic works in their hands which showed the same doctrine as the priest preached. The only answer to this was that the minister *had taken an oath to oppose " Popery" where ever he met with it, and let them say what they liked he would oppose it.* It was something to have a whole congregation of Presbyterian defenders. It is impossible to say what the results of all this might have been. The presence of the priest was required by the Bishops at Edinburgh, where he was appointed chaplain to the newly-established sisterhood, the *Ursulines de Jesus*, and preacher at St. Mary's church. The solemn service of Vespers had been for some time established at St. Mary's church. But as yet the attendance was very inconsiderable. The Bishop, although he had given up the charge of Edinburgh to his coadjutor, concurred with him in his endeavour to increase the attendance at Vespers. He presided pontifically every Sunday; and when he could not be present, the coadjutor took his place. He also gave all encouragement to the chaplain of the Ursulines, who undertook and announced a course of sermons on the doctrines of the Church to be delivered on Sunday afternoons at Vespers. There was also a very competent choir under the direction of Mr. Hargitt. In a few weeks the attendance was so much improved that the church was completely filled from the sanctuary rails to the door. This better state of things gave so much satisfaction to the Bishop that the coadjutor took occasion to compliment the congregation in a formal address from the altar.

Charitable and educational institutions were fostered by the Bishop and his colleague. Among these was a branch of the Ursuline community established in the heart of the "old town," whose care it was to teach the poorer children and also to visit and tend the sick poor; the Society of St. Vincent of Paul in the guidance of which the Rev. James Stothert took a leading part; and the Guild of St. Joseph which owed its origin to Bishop Gillis. This last named institution, modeled according to the ancient Catholic guilds, was efficient in providing mutual aid and exercising charity. It did good service, moreover, on occasions of religious processions, by its imposing numbers and the picturesque costume of its members. The Bishops extended their encouragement to the Catholic schools generally; and greatly promoted education among the poor by their attention to the "united industrial schools." These schools were first established at Edinburgh, under the name of "ragged schools," by a distinguished Protestant preacher, the Rev. Dr. Guthrie, for the benefit of his poorer parishioners. Then followed the Catholic "ragged schools," and, finally, both came to be united as "The United Industrial Schools" of Edinburgh. St. Margaret's Society was chiefly instituted in order to aid the poorer schools of the district. To it, also, the Bishops lent their countenance in concurrence with its principal founder, the late Mr. Monteith of Carstairs. The College of Blairs shared the solicitude of the Bishops; and the senior Bishop resided there for a considerable time, his example inspiring the students with a love for scientific study.

The Bishop was endowed with great literary taste. His knowledge of the ancient and modern classics was more than ordinary. He wrote Latin with elegance and spoke French with remarkable fluency, although he had never visited France since the time of his studies. He was also a patron of letters as well as of science. He rejoiced in the literary acquirements and oratorical powers of his eloquent coadjutor; and he often expressed his satisfaction with the controversial writings of the Rev. Paul McLachlan,

D. D., of Falkirk, who was a distinguished founder of missions and builder of churches, no less that with the writings of the Rev. Stephen Keenan, D.D., of Dundee, and those of the Rev. John Stewart McCorry, D. D., of Perth. With the Rev. Mr. Keenan and the Rev. John McPherson, D. D., the Bishop concurred in promoting the establishment of an academy at Welburn, near Dundee.

Among the many things that tended to give lustre to the pontificate of Bishop Carruthers were the discovery and final restoration to Scotland of that invaluable relic, the quigrich or crozier of St. Fillan. This relic is certainly the most interesting that remains in connection with ancient Scottish history. The late Mr. Adam Dawson was the first who aroused attention in regard to it, and made known that it had found its way to Canada. When visiting in the township of Beckwith he was shown the venerable quigrich together with documents which proved its authenticity, at the house of its hereditary guardian Alexander Dewar or Doir. He lost no time in communicating the information thus received to his brother the Rev. Æneas McDonell Dawson, LL. D., F. R. S., who was at the time resident at Dunfermline. The latter imparted this knowledge of the quigrich to his good friend, Sir Daniel Wilson, L. L. D., and F. R. S., who was then secretary to the Society of Antiquaries of Scotland, and engaged in preparing his learned work, "The Pre-historic Annals of Scotland." It was received as a valuable contribution to that work and occupies one of its brightest pages. The quigrich is remarkable as having been the crozier of St. Fillan, who, in the eighth century, continued the work of St. Columba among the Scots and Picts. It was held in great veneration by King Robert Bruce, who had it in the tent in which he heard Mass and received the Holy Communion, before joining battle with Edward II. of England at Bannockburn. Immediately after the conflict the King returned to his tent in order to give thanks to Almighty God for the great victory which he had won. Anxious to make sure that the relics of St. Fillan were in the reliquary at the head of the crozier, destined to contain them, on examination, he found them not. He asked the Abbot of Inchaffray, their custodian, to account for their absence, and received for reply that it had been thought prudent to remove them before the battle to a place of safety. "What better place of safety," said the King, indignantly, to the affrighted Abbot, "than the army of your King?" and, depriving him of the guardianship, confided it to Malise Doir, the ancestor of the Dewars or Doirs of Canada, who had distinguished himself by good service in the great battle. The quigrich continued under the guardianship of the Dewars till our day, with only a temporary interruption, when it came into the possession of the Catholic family of Glengarry. Mr. Dewar denied that it was parted with for money, as a common matter of bargain and sale; but admitted that it had been given in pledge for a loan. The Dewars ceasing to prosper from the time that they gave up the quigrich, appealed to the generosity of Glengarry, who liberally surrendered the precious relic to its hereditary guardians. Prosperity, however, did not return with the restoration of the sacred trust; and the family emigrated to Canada. Sir Daniel Wilson had also come to Canada, and was for some time a Professor in the University of which he is now the Principal. It was a cherished object with him to have the quigrich restored to Scotland. His first nogotiations with the Dewars proved fruitless. Some time later he returned to the charge and was more successful. Mr. Alex. Dewar himself had become anxious that the great relic should go back to Scotland. He was eighty-seven years of age; and rightly believed that his sons would not be guided by the same sentiments as himself in regard to Scotland and its historical associations. In fact, he could imagine the holy and historic relic among the profane shows of a Barnum or consigned to the melting pot. Such a fate could only be averted by treating with Sir Daniel Wilson; and he did so on the most liberal terms. Seven hundred dollars were the ransom for it required by the family. Two hundred of these Mr. Dewar himself agreed to pay. The rest was provided through Dr. Wilson, by the Society of Antiquaries at Edinburgh. It now remained only to have the venerable relic conveyed to Scotland. This Sir Daniel Wilson accomplished with complete success. A full meeting of the Antiquaries was held, the Marquess of Lothian presiding, on occasion of the reception of the quigrich which will ever remain as a sacred trust in the keeping of the venerable antiquaries, for the gratification, instruction and edification of Scotch people in all time to come. The most probable derivation of the name, quigrich, is from ("the king's crook") the crozier having been greatly venerated by King Robert Bruce. The deed, signed by Alex. Dewar and his son, Archibald, is dated December, 1876, and distinctly makes over in trust, to the Society of Antiquaries of Scotland the most interesting relic. (See "The proceedings of the Society of Antiquaries of Scotland, 97th session, 1876-1877, vol. 12; part 1". Edinburgh, 1877.)

CAP. LXIX.

CONVERSIONS—BISHOP GILLIS AND OTHER WRITERS—THE EX-KING OF FRANCE—DEATH OF MR. MENZIES—HIS LAST WILL—MAGNIFICENT FUNERAL—BISHOP GILLIS A DIPLOMATIST—HIS SUCCESS IN OBTAINING FUNDS FOR THE MISSION—CAUSES THE LIBRARY OF THE SCOTCH COLLEGE AT PARIS TO BE REMOVED TO BLAIRS—DEATH OF THE HONOURABLE AND RIGHT REVEREND ALEXANDER M'DONELL AT DUMFRIES—HIS FUNERAL AT EDINBURGH—IN 20 YEARS HIS REMAINS TRANSFERRED TO KINGSTON—THE CHURCH AND HOUSE OF ST. MARY'S, EDINBURGH, GREATLY IMPROVED—GUILD OF ST. JOSEPH—SOCIETY OF ST. VINCENT OF PAUL—BISHOP GILLIS AND THE "FREE CHURCH"—NEGOTIATIONS CONCERNING THE SCOTCH MONASTERY AT RATISBON—FINAL DECISION—FRENCH ROYAL FAMILY AT EDINBURGH—THE COUNT DE CHAMBORD—RELICS OF SAINT CRESCENTIA—RELICS OF SAINT MARGARET—PERTH BANQUET AT BIRTH OF THE PRINCESS ROYAL, 1840—GREAT PROGRESS, CONSOLING TO THE BISHOP IN HIS OLD AGE—HIS DEATH.

Conversions were not as yet very frequent in Scotland. That they were not impossible, however, circumstances occasionally showed. Towards the close of Bishop Carruthers' career, in the year 1850, Viscount Fielding came to Edinburgh in order to be received into the Church, together with Lady Fielding. They applied to the coadjutor Bishop, before whom they made their abjuration. This had scarcely been done when the Viscount's father, the Earl of Denbigh, accompanied by his chaplain, the Rev. Mr. Baylee, arrived, in the hope of being able to prevent his son and daughter-in-law from taking what he considered a false step. To his great mortification, however, it was too late. As if to make amends he and his clerical friend sought and obtained an interview with Bishop Gillis, at which Mr. Baylee raised a discussion on several tenets of the Catholic Church. The conversation, or controversy, lasted three hours; but led to no result. Soon after, Mr. Baylee published a very unfair account of the interview in the *Morning Herald*. Bishop Gillis was obliged, in consequence, to insert in the same paper a counter statement for his own vindication. An unprofitable newspaper correspondence was the result. But it was not of long continuance. It lasted, however, long enough to show how little justice was to be expected from the public press of the time. The unfairness of the *Herald's* report imposed on Bishop Gillis the necessity of publishing a pamphlet, in which he gave in detail the facts and arguments that had been brought forward, This work, although it had no effect on the opinions and prejudices of Mr. Baylee and his right houourable patron, was circulated, along with the coadjutor's other learned writings, and won for him, apart from his episcopal character, a high place among men of letters.

Another able writer of the time among Catholics was the Reverend James Stothert, a graduate of Cambridge and a convert to the Catholic faith. Of Mr. Stothert's ability as a writer and lecturer we need no better proof than the elegant lectures which he delivered at Edinburgh, and which gave so much delight to all who heard them.

Mr. William Turnbull, a member of the Edinburgh bar, was well known in those times as a man of letters and a zealous antiquary. He was for some time secretary to the Society of Antiquaries of Scotland; and was succeeded in that office by Principal Sir Daniel Wilson, now at Toronto. Mr. Turnbull, like Mr. Stothert, was a convert to the Catholic religion. Dr. Kemp, of the medical profession, was also a convert, and did honour to his profession by the elegance of his writings. Another convert, Sir William Drummond Stewart, was one of the first who travelled through and explored the Rocky Mountains of America, and was well known throng h out those wild regions as "the hospitable Scotchman." What he wrote about his travels entitles him to honourable mention among literary men. His nice appreciation of the fine arts was well shown in the tasteful decorations and whole style of the elegant chapel which, at a cost of £16,000, he erected near his family mansion, Murthly Castle.

Mr. Clerk, son of Sir George Clerk, Bart., of Pennycuick, so long known in Canada as the editor of the Montreal "*True Witness*," and much distinguished by his able writings, was a convert of the time. James Browne, LL.D., who so well illustrated portions of Scottish history, and who was also a convert to the Catholic Faith, fills, and is well entitled to fill, a high place among the literary characters of Edinburgh. The brothers, Alexander and George Miller, of the British army, grandsons of Lord Glenlea of the Court of Session (the Supreme Court of Scotland), and sons of Colonel Miller, who fell at Waterloo, are well entitled to an honourable place among the distinguished converts of the period.

If correct, elegant and judicious composition of sermons can give any claim to literary reputation, it eminently belonged to the Rev. Alexander Badenoch. It is to be regretted that he left no writing to impart instruction and perpetuate his memory. The ex-King of France, Charles X, who attended regularly at St. Mary's Church, where Mr. Badenoch was the senior priest, was heard to say that he showed much feeling in his sermons. Mr. Smith, editor of the *Catholic Magazine* of those times, and the first that appeared, must not be forgotten. His work ably promoted the cause of letters as well as that of religion. It would be a grievous mistake not to mention the venerable John Sharpe who after having laboured long in the mission, was President of Blairs' College in Bishop Carruthers' time. Under his rule, and without the aid of punishments, the highest discipline prevailed.

The Reverend William Bennet was one of the gifted men of Bishop Carruthers' time. He laboured many years in the mission, and was distinguished for both piety and learning. He joined the Society of Oblates and was Professor of Greek and English Literature for several years in the University which that Society founded and conducts at Ottawa, Canada. He died there at the advanced age of 73 in 1887.

In the time of Bishop Carruthers' that illustrious scholar, Nicholas Cardinal Wiseman, paid several visits to the clergy and Catholics of Edinburgh. Colonel McDonell of that time who lived long at Edinburgh, wrote a remarkable work, called "the Abrahamidæ," in which he endeavoured to prove that the people of Scotland are descended from the

Patriarch, Abraham. His work and the idea it maintains were only known to the Colonel's private friends, as he never published it,

Charles Glendonwyne Scott was a striking figure in the society of those days. He was called and was in reality, Mr. O'Connell's "Head Pacificator for Scotland." The mission lost its best benefactor when John Menzies, Esq., of Pitfodels, departed this life on the 11th of Oct., 1843. Bishop Gillis returned from an intended tour to Germany in time for the funeral, which was conducted with all the pomp becoming a friend of the Church who was so deeply lamented. Bishops Kyle and Murdoch were present, together with many of the clergy from various parts of Scotland. The Guild brethren, in full costume, appearing in procession from St. Mary's Church to the Chapel of St. Margaret's Convent, where the interment took place, added much to the solemnity of the services. Meanwhile, some of the populace mistook the brethren for priests; and certain murmurings were heard about so many "Romish" priests being in the city. This may not have amounted to much. Nevertheless, the police officers thought it advisable that the Guild men should not return in their uniform, and counselled them accordingly. Bishop Carruthers was unavoidably absent, being from home and not having had notice in time. Mr. Menzies' testamentary settlements had been partly executed in 1834. To St. Margaret's Convent he bequeathed a considerable sum of money, together with a small landed estate, for the benefit of the community established there. Bishop Gillis he appointed his residuary legatee, and willed to him, besides, the property and house of Greenhill, where Mr. Menzies had spent the last years of his life, and, along with it, the plate and furniture. The library also, he left to the Bishop during his life, appointing that it should afterwards belong to the future College of the Eastern District. The testator directed, moreover, that the debts of the two churches of Edinburgh should be paid out of his funds. Legacies were left to each of the three Vicars-Apostolic for building new churches in the Highland portions of the Western district, and for erecting a new church at Aberdeen. In addition there were several bequests to individuals; so that almost the whole of Mr. Menzies' property was devised for ecclesiastical and charitable purposes in Scotland.

Soon after the appointment and consecration of Dr. Gillis as coadjutor, Bishop Carruthers had good reason to congratulate himself on the diplomatic ability and success of the newly appointed Bishop in obtaining additional funds for the use of the mission. Hitherto the Society for the Propagation of the

Faith, which originated at Lyons in 1822, and had one of its directing councils at Paris, had confined its benefactions to missions outside of Europe. When Bishop Gillis applied for some aid to the struggling missions of Scotland the reply was given that the Society could not deviate from the purpose for which it was founded, even in favour of the poorest European mission. The Bishop was not to be defeated. Availing himself of his acquaintance in France, and finding himself sustained in his views by several religious and influential persons, he set about establishing another charitable society for giving assistance in European missionary countries, on the same plan as that of the institution already in existence. In this endeavour he was eminently successful. The devout Catholics, who at first favoured his views, and lent him their countenance, continuing to sustain him, the new institution, called *l'œuvre du Catholicism en Europe* (the work of Catholicity in Europe), was established at Paris. The prospects of this undertaking were in a short time so good that the first Society became alarmed for its prosperity. Its councils, dreading the influence of the rival institution, laid the whole case before the Holy See. It was there decided that there should be only one society, as the interests of two rival societies might often clash and injure each other. It would tend more to promote the general good, that the missions of all countries, whether European or other, should in future, receive aid in proportion to the necessities of each mission and the means at command of the Society for granting aid. It was, no doubt, cause of regret that a good work with such excellent prospects, should be abandoned. Meanwhile, it had produced its fruit. The council of the original, or rather, the united society entertained favourably the case of the Scotch missions, and ever since they have shared abundantly in its distributions.

The influence of the coadjutor was still further employed in obtaining that all that remained of the library of the Scotch College of Paris, should be transferred to Blairs. In May, 1839, he returned to Scotland.

A singularly distinguished son of Scotland, where were spent the earlier years of his ecclesiastical career, justly claims honourable mention here. Urged by his sacerdotal zeal the Honourable and Right Rev. Alexander McDonell, of Kingston, had traversed the Atlantic Ocean and revisited the scenes of his earlier labours in order to obtain some assistance for his recently established diocese in Canada, It was not however, the will of the Great Master that he should continue his work in the vineyard; and he was called suddenly to his reward a day or two after his arrival at Dumfries, in Scotland, on the 14th day of January, 1840. (For details see Biography by Chevalier W. J. McDonell, of Toronto, Canada.) It was resolved, on the occasion, to do the greatest possible honour, as was fitting in the case of a prelate who had been so eminent in his day as a Bishop, and, in trying times, had done signal service to both Church and State. The remains were conveyed to Edinburgh in order to be temporarily deposited in the vaults of the chapel of St. Margaret's Convent. The funeral services were conducted with extraordinary pomp at St. Mary's Church. Nothing of the kind so splendid had been seen at Edinburgh since Royalty ceased to have its abode in the Scottish capital. A magnificent funeral car was provided, a procession formed, and all that was mortal of the great Bishop conveyed to the Convent, there to await transference to the seat of his Canadian diocese. Twenty years later one of his successors, Bishop Horan, effected the change and laid down in their final resting place the remains of Kingston's first Bishop.

When Bishop Carruthers gave over the charge of Edinburgh and its two churches to his coadjutor, the latter made several improvements in St. Mary's Church. The pews were in great part renewed. A new altar with appropriate furniture, and a new pulpit were erected. A screen of elaborately carved oak was placed at great cost around the sanctuary, and within it an episcopal throne and a choir organ. The chief organ, meanwhile, was repaired and enlarged, and the church newly painted and decorated within. The house in which resided the Bishop and clergy was also considerably improved. The walls were raised a few feet and new furniture provided.

It was at this time also that Dr. Gillis, with the consent of the Bishop, instituted the Holy Guild of St. Joseph. Ii was his good fortune also to favour the establishing in Edinburgh of the well known Society of St. Vincent of Paul. This brotherhood that followed so closely in the footsteps of its sainted patron, although it originated in Paris so late as 1833, in a short time had branches all over France, and somewhat later, in every country where there are Catholics. At Edinburgh there are three conferences.

At this time (1846), Mr. Frederick Monod, a Calvinist minister, directed, under the auspices of the Free Church of Scotland, a volume of calumnies and misrepresentations against the Catholic Church. The Bishop considered it his duty to reply. He accordingly, prepared an elaborate refutation of Mr. Monod's book and addressed it to the assembly of the Free Church, which was then in session. No answer was received, and it is not known what impression the Bishop's work produced on the Free Church mind; but the volume remains a monument of its author's learning, moderation and literary skill.

Bishop Carruthers, at his advanced age, could ill dispense, even temporarily, with the presence at Edinburgh and aid of his coadjutor. It was, nevertheless, resolved that the latter should proceed to Ratisbon in Bavaria, as representative of the Vicars-Apostolic of Scotland, in order to obtain if possible, that on the decease of the last Scotch Benedictine, Prior Deasson (Dawson,) the Monastery of St. James should be secularized and converted into a Seminary for the Scotch missions. Such a demand was not unreasonable, as all the properties connected with the Monastery, had been gifted to it by Scotchmen, noblemen and others interested in the cause of Scotch education. The Bishop had taken care to provide himself with letters of introduction from the ex-Royal Family of France. He succeeded, moreover, in interesting in favour of his view the Bishop of Ratisbon and the surviving Religious. He then repaired to Munich and obtained an audience of the King, who received him with favour, entertained his application, and referred him for a final answer to his Minister for Ecclesiastical Affairs. It appears to have been no easy matter for this Minister to manufacture a reply. For it was not given till after a delay of four months, when everything asked for was refused, and a threat held out, at the same time, that if the Monastery were not supplied with subjects, Scotch Benedictines, within six months, it would be delivered to Bavarian members of the same Order. The Bishop replied to this extraordinary State paper, which was wholly founded on erroneous assumptions, in a memorial which was called "Reclamations," and which set forth the claims and rights of the Scotch mission to the whole property, proving beyond question, that it was the intention of the founders and benefactors to promote the cause of the Catholic Religion in Scotland, and not to benefit the Bavarians. He pointed out, moreover, how unjust it would be to alienate the Seminary from the Scotch mission, declaring it to be nothing less than an act of spoliation. The Bavarian Ministry were proof against argument. Meanwhile, Bishop Gillis submitted the memorial to Lord Palmerston, at the time Foreign Secretary, and requested him to use his influence with the Court of Bavaria in order to obtain more reasonable terms. The British Minister promised to give his aid and suggested that the memorial should be presented to him in a more condensed form. This was done; and the Government, through their envoy at at Munich, Mr. Milbank, made a representation to the Bavarian Ministry. This action was not without its effect. The threatened measure was suspended, and the matter in question was referred for final decision to the Holy See. There even, the niggardly spirit of the Bavarian Ministry so far prevailed that only £10,000 was allowed to Scotland in lieu of all the properties bestowed by Scotchmen on the Monastery of St. James of Ratisbon. It was a condition of this decision that the sum mentioned should be applied in aid of additions to the Scotch College at Rome. The negotiations lasted eight months, the two or three last of which the Bishop spent at Bruges. In March, 1849, he returned to Edinburgh.

The pontificate of Bishop Carruthers was further illustrated by the sojourn for some years, at Edinburgh of the ex-King, Charles X., and the exiled Royal Family of France. All kind and proper attentions were shown them by the Bishop, his coadjutor, the Rev. Alexander Badenoch, and the other priests of the time. A special pew was fitted up for them in St. Mary's Church, where they regularly attended, and a private passage opened from the Bishop's house to the church.

The grandson and heir of the exiled King Henri, Duc De Bordeaux, better known, afterwards, as Count De Chambord, had his earlier education at Edinburgh. Later in life, when a young man, he revisited the scenes of his youth in Scotland. He was treated everywhere with attention and every mark of regard. He paid a visit to St. Margaret's Convent, and held a levee there attended by His Grace, Mgr. le Duc De Lévis, Admiral Count Villaret Joyeuse and his preceptor, M. De Barande. Several persons of distinction friends of his family availed themselves of the opportunity to honour him with their friendly greetings. The chaplain, who as such, and also as senior priest of Edinburgh, assisted the good sisters in doing the honours of the house, in the absence of the Bishop, requested Mgr. De Lévis to present to the Prince, the venerable Sister Agnes Xavier, informing him that she was the daughter of a Presbyterian clergyman, and a convert to the Catholic Faith, the first Scotch lady who, since the Religious Revolution, became a Religious, and one of the first colony of Religious Sisters who occupied St. Margaret's Convent. To hear all this was a new pleasure to the Prince, who was a good Catholic.

In 1842, a new honour was added to the pontificate of Bishop Carruthers by the arrival in Scotland of the relics of one of the early martyrs. This good fortune was due to the zeal of a Catholic lady, Mrs. Colonel Hutchison, who, on occasion of a visit to Rome, had an audience of the Holy Father, Gregory XVI., at which she was introduced as a convert from Protestantism, and a liberal benefactress of the Scotch missions. The Pope was so pleased that he asked her to name any favour it might be in his power to grant. The good lady expressed her wish to obtain the relics of a saint for her "eldest daughter." On learning that this was no other than Saint Margaret's Convent, Gregory XVI. immediately ordered that the body of Saint Crescentia, Virgin and Martyr, should be confided to Mrs. Hutchison. On her return home, in company with Bishop Ullathorne, she was arrested at Leghorn, having been mistaken for a person of the same name who had aided in the escape of Lavalette in 1816. Bishop Ullathorne on reaching London, drew up a statement of the case, which was presented to Lord Aberdeen by Lord Cunningham, (a Judge of the Supreme Court) Mrs. Hutchison's brother. The British Minister lost no time in communicating with Prince Metternich, and an apology speedily put an end to the trouble. A list of "contraband" individuals was no longer kept on the frontier of Lombardy, where many British travellers had been stopped and turned back. In future there could be no such annoyance. The case of relics which Mrs. Hutchison carried with her was an additional source of anxiety to her during her misadventure. She succeeded, however, in bringing it safely to Edinburgh; and the relics of Saint Crescentia, having been duly presented to the Ursuline Sisterhood, were deposited in an elegant shrine, designed by the celebrated architect, Pugin, and manufactured by Bonnar and Carfrae, of Edinburgh.

Somewhat later, Scotland and the Convent were enriched with a relic of Queen Saint Margaret, obtained from Spain through the exertions of Bishop Gillis, when Vicar-Apostolic. But we must not anticipate.

One of the latest acts of the Bishop, now far advanced in years, was to preside at the re-opening of the enlarged and improved Church of St. John, at Perth. He asked on that occasion the writer, who had preached in the forenoon, to give a second sermon at the Vesper service. On the latter suggesting that it would be more acceptable to the congregation to hear a few words from their Bishop, the aged prelate addressed to them a short but very feeling allocution. In connection with Perth it may be mentioned, as shewing the advancing liberality of the time, that on occasion of a banquet given by the municipality, 1840, in honour of the birth of the Princess Royal, now Empress Dowager of Germany, the Lord Provost invited the priest in charge at the time, and included him in the toast of *the clergy*, to the great satisfaction of the numerous company.

It was a source of great consolation to the venerable Bishop in his declining years, to observe the progress which religion had made during his comparatively short pontificate. The number of churches and clergy had increased and was still increasing; the cause of Catholic education was daily gaining ground; Catholics from being a disliked and dreaded sect, were become popular; religious societies had begun to be introduced; the community of St. Margaret's, with its two houses, had gained by its successful pains in the work of education and its charitable care of the sick, the affection of the Catholics and the esteem of the general public. The Bishop was now eighty-three years of age, and having lived to witness all that he could expect or hope for, he was prepared to say, like the saintly Simeon, "*Now, O Lord, dismiss Thy servant in peace, for my eyes have seen the advance of Thy salvation.*" He was still active, however, and persevered in visiting the missions; insomuch, that it was remarked that he thought he could never do enough of duty. His last visit was to Dunfermline, the chief seat of the Fifeshire missions, which he had caused to be founded. He was there the guest of the writer for the better part of a day; and after an early dinner returned to Edinburgh, apparently in his usual good health. He had scarcely reached the capital, however, when he was attacked with typhus fever, which, in its fatal course of eleven days, put an end to his career, but not until after he had participated in all the consolations of religion and set a bright example of Christian fortitude and patience. His death was generally lamented and spoken of in the public prints as that of the "the much beloved prelate."

THE END.

ADDENDA.

TULLOCH-ALLUM.

Tulloch-Allum in the Highlands of Banffshire, alluded to in this work, was a favourite resort of the venerable Bishop Hay. The head of the family that had been resident there for several generations was devoted to the Bishop always served his mass and accompanied him on his missionary journeyings. His eldest son, John Gordon, who was studying for the priesthood at the College of Douai at the time of the French Revolution, escaped from France, along with other students, and became distinguished as a missionary Priest. He built a church at Dumbarton and another at Greenock, where, afterwards, the late Reverend William Gordon, the last chief of the clan Gordon of Glenbucket, was so long the zealous and popular pastor.

The following account of the missions of Cabrach, Achendoune, and Abuline Speyside, from 1770 till 1856, has been furnished by a worthy member of the family so long resident at Tullochallum. The priest or missionary for the time resided mostly at Shenval, parish of Cabrach, one of the coldest spots in that poor country. A very humble thatched cottage was the church—long ago levelled to the ground.

The Catholics in Cabrach were few and poor, but, like the other missions, were protected by the powerful Duke of Gordon.

At Achendoune, in those days they had no church. Mass was said there at intervals at the farm of Tullochallum, then occupied by John Gordon, a cadet and near relative of Gordon of Cairnfield in the Enzie, already mentioned in these sketches, and still in the possession of his grandson, George Gordon. No room in the modest house of Tullochallum was large enough for the few Catholics, so that mass was celebrated in the "kiln." A complete set of hangings to cover the temporary altar were kept at Tullochallum; and one of the sons, principally the late Alexander Gordon, had the honour of carrying the altar stone and chalice, with other requisites for mass, from Shenval to Tullochallum and thence to Abuline, his duties further consisting of serving mass, the priest as a rule visiting each place in succession

There were few Catholics in Abuline, but the family, a cadet branch of the Letterfourie Gordons, were firmly attached to the old faith.

In addition to this, Bishop Hay, when on his journeys between Aberdeen and Scalan, invariably spent some time at Tullochallum, resting occasionally a few weeks, his episcopal Palace for the time being what in the language of those days was termed "the guest chamber," a room or rooms apart from the main house. Here in quiet and solitude he used to write part of those works so long famous in Scotland, and forming to this day what his worthy successor, the late Rev. Bishop Kyle, justly styled "The Layman's Theology." When on his journeys, always performed in his later years on horseback, the bishop was accompanied by a man servant. This was necessary, as well for assistance as protection, as they carried all the baggage, including the bishop's vestments and everything necessary for celebrating mass, in two immense saddle...

The bishop, his man, and horses were welcome at Tullochallum so long as they chose to remain. It was mainly to the charity and generosity of John Gordon, ably supported by his pious spouse, a near relative of Gordon of Glenbucket, that the mission of Achendoune owed its life and existence.

Both from the fact that it was frequently the temporary home of Bishop Hay, as well as the resting place of every priest travelling that way, the name of Tullochallum was so well known at Rome that some of the students on their return to Scotland as priests, having heard so much of it and the family, were astonished to find it was only a modest farm house.

The late John Gordon was often heard to remark (he was himself a very early riser, never in bed after four o'clock) that on going to visit the bishop—the first thing he did every morning—he never found His Lordship in bed or asleep, but on his knees at prayer.

When times became less intolerant, and it was considered more convenient for priest and people, the headquarters of the mission were removed from Shenval to the farm of Upper Keithock in Achendoune, possibly about 1790. To help the priest to live the Duke of Gordon rented him the small farm; and a little church was built, one story and thatched roof. The priest then was a Mr. Davidson, a native of the Enzie. John Gordon of Tullochallum took upon himself the cost of cultivating the priest's farm, seed, and labor—never doing a thing for his own till the priest's crop was laid down.

Rev. Mr. Davidson was removed from there to Greenock and was succeeded early in this century by the Rev. George Gordon, a native of Garioch, Aberdeen-shire, in many ways a remarkable man. Educated at the Scotch College in Valladolid he was a thorough Spaniard to the end of his life; a born musician, as his masses and hymns testify; composed and arranged for the use of small choirs as their title sets forth, they are to this day the standard music in many missions in Scotland, as much as Bishop Hay works were the theology of the people.

Mr. Gordon, not satisfied with the thatched chapel, set to work and erected a comfortable two story stone building, still date. The lower story served as the presbytery and the upper, having a vaulted roof, made a very respectable chapel—a great improvement on the other with the mud floor.

In 1817 the village of Dufftown on the property of the Earl of Fife, a very liberal nobleman, was begun. It is situated about two and a half miles north-west of the farm of Upper Keithock and, besides being more central was on the highway to Glenlivat and the upper missions. Mr. Gordon got a grant of a few acres of land from the Earl of Fife, and in 1825 he built thereon a neat stone church with gothic facade, in dressed sandstone as well as a compact and comfortable presbytery, also in stone, and enclosed the whole property with a stone and lime wall, all of which remain to this day a standing memorial of his zeal and energy.

With his taste and his musical talent he got an organ for the new church, and trained several members of his choir, male and female, to play and sing. Some years before his death in 1856 he, out of his private means, purchased a magnificent organ, costing about one thousand pounds sterling, and presented it to the mission, the smaller organ going to another place.

This good and pious priest lies buried at the side of the altar in the church his zeal was the means of erecting, and a marble tablet in the hall records a fitting tribute to his memory. How little many now alive, and in this over-busy century, think how much they are indebted to the zeal, piety and self-denial of their ancestors who in sad days of trial kept for them the inestimable gift of the Catholic faith!

PROGRESS.

In order to convey an idea of the growth of the church since the restoration of the hierarchy, it may be mentioned that in the Archdiocese of Glasgow alone, the number of Catholics has increased to 220,000.

The work of education keeps pace with the increase of population. The teaching staff of the Archdiocese numbers 679. There has been an extraordinary extension of mission schools from 1877 to 1888. Accommodation augmented from 23,911 to 34,612; number on rolls from 21,647 to 33,283; average attendance from 14,521 to 24,292; number presented at Government examination from 10,655 to 23,117; at religious examination from 16,599 to 26,477; while at the other schools the accommodation has risen from 1739 to 2082; number on rolls from 1508 to 1679; the number presented at religious examination from 1220 to 1553.

A second synod of the Archdiocese of Glasgow was held in October last, the Archbishop presiding and 120 priests attending. The decrees of the first National Council which had been held at Fort Augustus were promulgated and the appointment announced of "Missionary Rectors" for thirteen missions.

DeMAISTRE'S CELEBRATED
SOIRÉES DE ST. PETERSBURG.

At $2.00.

Orders to be sent to the author of " The Catholics of Scotland."

IT is not pretended that the "Soirees de St. Petersburg," the last production of the illustrious author, are superior to his book on the Pope. Both are the work of genius. Both are, in our estimation, beautiful. Nevertheless, however the latter work may be admired, we doubt not that the former will have a still greater number of admirers. In his treatise on the Pope, M. de Maistre develops only one truth. In order to place this one truth in its fullest light, he employs all the resources of his talent, he lavishes all the treasures of his learning. In the work before us the field is more extensive, or, to speak more truly, without limits. He considers man in all his relations with God. He undertakes to reconcile free will with Divine power. He aims at unfolding the great enigma of good and evil. He takes possession of innumerable truths, or rather of all great and useful truths, as having a right to them. In order to defend them, as their legitimate possessor, against pride and impiety by which they have been all attacked. Never did the abject philosophy of the 18th century meet with a more formidable adversary. He is not awed by systems, by genius or celebrated names. He advances without interruption, demolishing as he proceeds all these colossal statues with feet of clay. Never did man search with more sagacity the tortuous folds of sophistry, drag it to the light and exhibit it, such as it is, absurd or ridiculous. Never was more extensive and more varied erudition employed with more art and judgment in order to corroborate argument with all the power of evidence.

By the author of "The Catholics of Scotland."

PIUS IX. AND HIS TIME

440 Pages.

At $1.50 ; Strongly Bound $2.00.

"THE BEST WORK ON THE SUBJECT IN THE ENGLISH LANGUAGE."
Monthly Magazine, London, England.

Orders as above ; or Thomas Coffey, London, Ontario, Canada
EUROPEAN EDITION.—Thos. Baker, 1 Soho Sq., London, Eng.

JUST PUBLISHED
THE
"CATHOLICS OF SCOTLAND"
By the REV. Æ. McD. DAWSON, LL.D., F.R.

Thomas Coffey, Catholic Record Office, London, Ont.
Thomas Baker, 1 Soho Square, London, England.

1890.

www.ingramcontent.com/pod-product-compliance
Lighting Source LLC
Chambersburg PA
CBHW020826230426
43666CB00007B/1114